Beginner's Guide
to Aquaponics

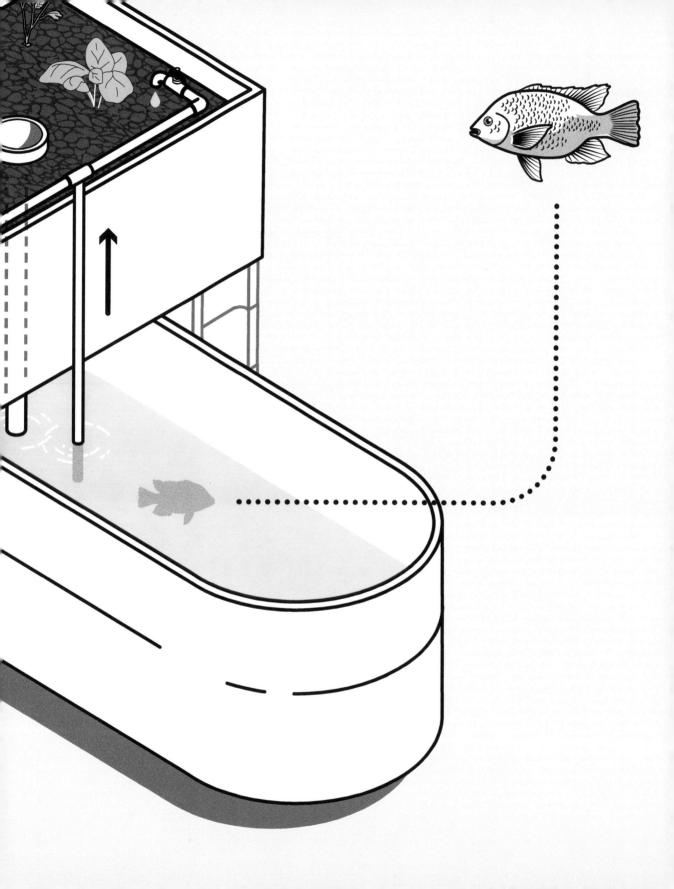

BEGINNER'S GUIDE
TO
AQUAPONICS

STEP-BY-STEP SYSTEMS
FOR PLANTS AND FISH

Seth Connell

ROCKRIDGE
PRESS

For general information on our other products and services or to obtain technical support, please contact our Customer Care Department within the United States at (866) 744-2665, or outside the United States at (510) 253-0500.

Rockridge Press publishes its books in a variety of electronic and print formats. Some content that appears in print may not be available in electronic books, and vice versa.

Interior and Cover Designer: Eric Pratt

Art Producer: Meg Baggott

Editor: Arturo Conde

Production Editor: Rachel Taenzler

Illustrations © Kay Coenen, 2020

ISBN: Print 978-1-64739-748-7
eBook 978-1-64739-450-9
R0

This book is dedicated to you, the evolving aquaponic gardener. Everyone in the industry started right where you are, by picking up a book to learn more. It is my earnest hope that this text will help you start, grow, and enjoy your life with aquaponics.

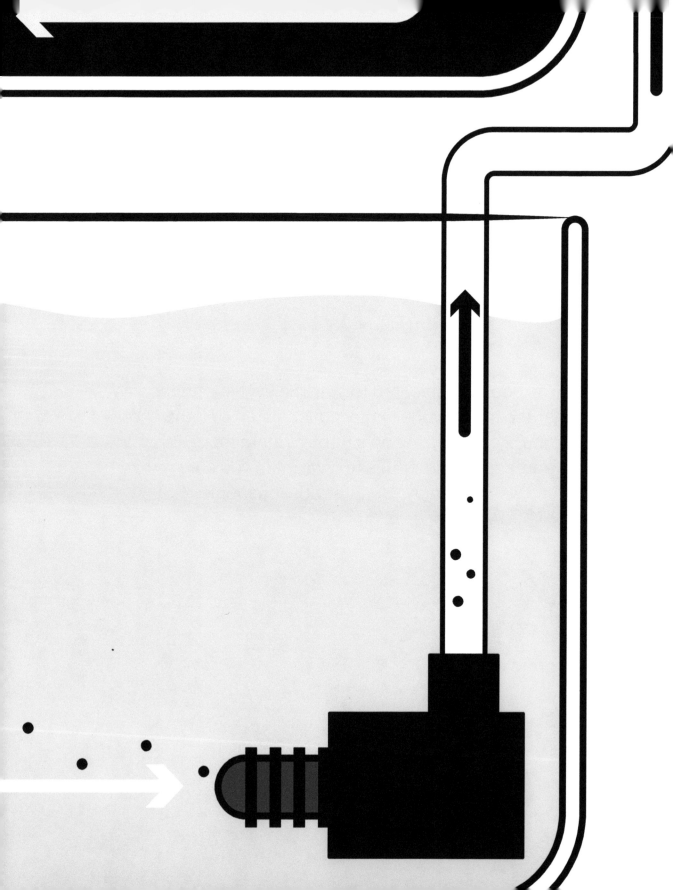

Contents

Introduction

Smart Farming with Plants and Fish

Aquaponics is an agricultural practice with ancient roots that holds great promise for a future where self-sufficiency is becoming the new status quo. While the earliest evidence is disputed, research suggests that aquaponics appeared independently in three distinct places: China, Central America, and Hawai'i. To this day, the Chinese practice terraquaculture, in which fish fertilize rice growing in shallow terraced ponds. The Aztecs of Central America created floating rafts called chinampas that cultivated a variety of plants with fish fertilizer. Ancient Hawai'ians also used fish in their ahupua'a food systems to fertilize their lo'i ponds for growing taro. All of these cultures cultivated plants and fish together because it works remarkably well.

Most old-world agrarian societies spent thousands of years focused on the popular yet less sustainable methods of slash-and-burn farming and growing commodity crops for trade. Those who found harmony in primal aquaponic methods gained the added benefit of using fewer resources to grow more food for their people. Oral histories and traditions preserved this valuable knowledge, while the second and third agricultural revolutions completely transformed agrarian societies into the world that we have today.

Even though those popular farming methods evolved into industrial agriculture that has left us with only 11 percent arable land remaining to farm, our civilization has been able to merge technology with tradition to create a remedy: modern aquaponics. We no longer rely on geographic location, weather patterns, and the cycle of seasons to plan our crops. Today we use greenhouses, warehouses, and environmental controls to conduct biomimicry and recreate ecosystems from any part of the world. This allows us to grow practically any plant, anywhere, anytime with far fewer resources, which reduces our impact on the planet and the animals we share it with.

Over the course of my career, I have gained a wealth of knowledge and experience in growing all kinds of things. From researching archaeo-agriculture as an undergraduate student to working on commercial aquaponic farms in Hawai'i and consulting for multiple departments of agriculture, I've had the great fortune to learn from masters of the trade all around the globe. It has also been my privilege to share those lessons and teach sustainable agriculture to people just like you, all over the world. A taste of that knowledge is collected here to empower you, the budding aquapon, so you can use this smart farming method to improve your life and health.

In this book, I will walk you through the amazing food production method we call modern aquaponics. You will learn how the merging of hydroponics and fish farming has created a powerhouse production method that is changing the way we grow our food. In many ways, our journey is just beginning, for this sector of sustainable agriculture is relatively new and growing fast—quite literally! I will teach you the ins and outs of different systems, take you step-by-step through building different systems, and advise you on drafting action plans so you can get started on a successful aquaponic journey.

CHAPTER ONE

What Is Aquaponics?

Aquaponic systems create a self-sustaining ecosystem in which to raise plants and fish. They combine hydroponic systems, which grow plants without soil, and recirculating aquaculture systems, which raise fish and sometimes culture other organisms, too. The two systems work symbiotically: Waste from aquaculture systems is converted into nutrients for plants grown in hydroponic systems, solving two problems in each industry with a bright solution. The union of both systems is what we refer to as aquaponics.

In this chapter, we will explore how aquaponic systems work. You will learn about the benefits these systems bring not just to the grower, but also to the environment. This chapter will also give you a good idea of what you can reasonably expect from using a system yourself with regards to time, output, and cost.

Key Terms

- Aquapon
- Biomimicry
- Deep water culture (DWC)
- Dutch buckets
- Hybrid system
- Media bed
- Nitrifying bacteria
- Nutrient film technique (NFT)

- Principle of gravity
- Principle of recirculation
- Solids lifting outlet (SLO)
- Sump tank
- Vermicomposting
- Vertical tier
- Vertical tower
- Wicking bed

How Does It Work?

Aquaponic food systems get their fertilizer from fish instead of mammals. Using this natural nutrient source as opposed to synthetic options supports microorganism activity and increases biodiversity within the fertilizer. Plants can't absorb the nutrients in fish waste directly from the source. Aquaponic systems use beneficial **nitrifying bacteria** to facilitate a nitrogen cycle that turns fish urine into bioavailable nitrogen for the plants, while worms convert solid waste into other minerals for the roots to absorb.

Vermicomposting is the process of worms breaking down the solid fish waste into worm droppings called castings. As water flows through the system, this vermicompost gradually dissolves, creating what is referred to as a compost tea. (When made from fish waste, worm castings don't harbor pathogens that can infect humans. On the other hand, mammalian-derived castings may culture harmful bacteria like *E. coli* or contagious viruses. That's why the common mistake of adding store-bought compost tea to your system can introduce harmful microorganisms.)

Having strong beneficial bacterial colonies expedites this process and increases the number of nutrients available to your plants. If any residual nutrients remain after the tea water has made its way through the grow beds, it is recycled to ensure full absorption for maximized yields.

This **principle of recirculation** is simple yet profound. It's how we are able to use 5 to 10 percent of the water as soil farming to grow the same plants. Rather than waste both water and nutrients, aquaponic systems cycle the water over and over. This ensures that 90 to 95 percent of the water will be absorbed by the plants you grow. Any water lost is attributed solely to evaporation and plant absorption.

Incorporating the **principle of gravity** in system design helps in many ways. Imagine the pump as an elevator that quickly lifts water instead of people. The water exits at the top and, as if walking downstairs, slowly flows down through tiered grow beds. At the bottom, the water is once again pumped back to the top so the cycle can repeat *ad infinitum*. It's important to remember that a body of water will always seek to level in between two or more containers when connected by a pipe or tube.

Typically, water begins in a fish tank where it gets fertilized. A pump then sends fish wastewater to either a series of filters or a media bed where bacteria and/or worms transform waste into bioavailable minerals, ensuring every opportunity for conversion. Plants in grow beds absorb the nitrogen, bioavailable minerals, and other dissolved nutrients to clean the water that is returned to the fish tank.

A **sump tank** is an optional collection basin at the very end of the flow that is common in larger systems. Sump tanks house the water pump, sending water up to the fish tank and/or grow beds. In these systems, a **solids lifting outlet (SLO)** drain in the fish tank directs solids and wastewater onward in the flow toward filters and grow beds via gravity. SLOs are pipes in the center of a fish tank with holes or slits in them, with a tee fitting at the top that is open to prevent draining the tank.

Plants are grown either exclusively in one style of grow bed or in many types, which is referred to as a **hybrid system**. Methods most commonly used to successfully grow plants include:

Deep water culture (DWC): These beds are large tables of aerated moving water. Rafts on the aerated water grow leafy greens.

Dutch buckets: These are like miniature media beds reserved for single fruiting plants, such as fruiting vines and bushes.

Media beds: Media beds house porous stones where bacteria and worms thrive, doubling as both a biofilter and a grow bed. Heavyweight media holds many types of plants in place.

Nutrient film technique (NFT): These beds use many separate channels or tubes with trickling water to grow leafy greens.

Vertical tiers: These use multiple levels of media beds or DWC to double or triple production.

Vertical towers: This modular method drips water down their insides to fertilize plants and increase production per square foot.

Wicking beds: These use two types of media to grow root crops, leafy greens, and herbs. Wicking beds are the only method where soil is viable in an aquaponic system, and are a unique spin on media-bed designs.

The goal for aquaponic practitioners is to create the same conditions our organisms require from their natural ecosystem in our own systems. This is called **biomimicry**: imitating an environmental system to the best of one's ability. By providing our organisms with appropriate atmospheric conditions, water chemistry, and light cycles, we maximize their potential in a controlled environment. With these principles combined, aquaponic systems can be powerful growing systems for any organism.

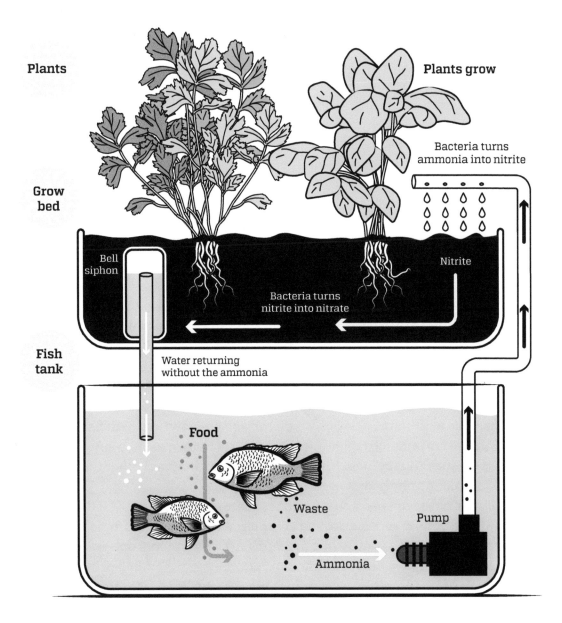

Plants

Plants grow

Grow bed

Bacteria turns ammonia into nitrite

Bell siphon

Nitrite

Bacteria turns nitrite into nitrate

Fish tank

Water returning without the ammonia

Food

Waste

Pump

Ammonia

What Are the Benefits?

When you give plants everything they need to grow—nutrients, water, and light—they tend to love it. Aquaponic practitioners know this all too well and are able to reap the rewards. High dissolved oxygen (DO) content in water expedites root production and nutrient uptake by creating aerobic conditions where beneficial bacteria flourish. Stable water-chemistry values keep all organisms in your system thriving. Regulated light cycles, frequencies, and intensity increase phytonutrient production, yield, flavors, and aromas. Whether growing indoors, outdoors, or in a greenhouse, there are many shared benefits of growing with aquaponic technology.

The most obvious advantage is being able to use 5 to 10 percent of the water, land, and labor as soil farming to grow the same food. Recirculating water keeps it in the system, so it is not wasted into the earth. Producing more dense crops at a faster pace means we can use at least 90 percent less land to grow a soil season's worth of food on a regular basis year-round. The amount of food grown on 100 square feet of soil in a typical 3-month season can be grown with aquaponics on 10 square feet and harvested year-round in weekly or daily intervals. By incorporating automated tools like timers or pumps, we also save time on labor.

Since aquaponic systems are not bound by the limitations of soil and climate, they can technically be set up anywhere in the world and designed to grow any crop, just like hydroponics does with plants and aquaculture with fish. The merging of these two practices solves the problems of both, making a simpler system. And because aquaponics eliminates weeding, tilling, and other menial soil tasks, it's easier on our bodies.

Probably the most advantageous benefit of these systems is their modularity and scalability to fit both residential and commercial needs. For example, some systems are small enough to outfit an aquarium with a functional one-to-one media bed for growing herbs on your kitchen counter with a goldfish providing the fertilizer. Scale up to a backyard system, and you may be able to effectively reduce grocery store expenses by growing enough produce for a small to medium-sized family.

Scaling up even larger opens up the possibility of starting a small business, growing for your local community, or even expanding to multiple facilities and selling to grocery stores. Most major cities are experiencing a trend of indoor agriculture overtaking warehouses and abandoned buildings. Soon, this idea will spread to the suburbs and rural communities. With the skills and technology to grow safe, uncontaminated food for people the world over, the future of farming is literally knocking at our door.

How Much Food Can You Produce?

While I could spout off some statistics on how much more food you can grow with aquaponics versus soil or hydro, there is no one-equation-fits-all number. What I've come to teach you is that it's not about the system you grow with so much as it is about you, the **aquapon** (short for aquaponic practitioner). Every aquapon requires proper training, planning, and a regular habitual maintenance routine that we will explore in chapter 6 (see page 111). Only then will you be able to grow food that is tastier than you imagine in quantities larger than you would expect, all in a time frame that is faster than you think.

One commonly quoted figure suggests 25 square feet of an aquaponic system can grow enough food for one person, but this is a myth. If one person grows only lettuce in that space, then sure, they will have plenty of lettuce every day. But that's not something you can derive all your nutrition from. You need to grow other plants, and their needs and growth times will differ from those of lettuce. Only in planning do we discover that some days you harvest crop A, on other days crops B and C, while on select days are you able to harvest all three. Only at a much larger scale can you reliably grow and harvest every crop, every day.

At base, you can produce the same food as a soil garden 10 times the size of your aquaponic system. Lettuce farmers, for instance, may have four 100-foot-long rows spaced one foot apart with lettuce planted eight inches from one another. This gives you 150 heads times four rows, resulting in 600 heads. Divided by 416 square feet, we have a density of 1.44 plants per square foot.

In a DWC system growing lettuce, we adjust the density over time. When we transplant mature seedlings to a floating raft, we can fill a 36-cell raft at 4.5 plants per square foot, allowing them to grow until the white of the raft isn't visible. After two weeks, we move them to a 28-cell raft at 3.5 plants per square foot until they are ready to harvest three to four weeks later. This comes out to four to six weeks per plant compared to six to twelve weeks in soil. Our rafts grow at an average density of 4 plants per square foot compared to 1.4 plants per square foot in soil, already a 280 percent advantage.

If we want to match the soil farm's production of 600 heads per year, then we have some math to do. Since aquaponics focuses on a reliable weekly harvest, we will divide 600 by 52 to discover we want to grow 11.5 heads per week; let's round up to 12. In a worst-case scenario where we could only order 28-cell rafts, then only half a raft would be needed each week. If these plants took six weeks to grow in our rafts, then we end up using three rafts in total, transplanting half a raft every week.

Each raft measures 8 square feet. When multiplied by three, we get 24 square feet. That's right: We only need 24 square feet of DWC to grow 416 square feet worth of soil lettuce. In this case, that's only 6 percent of the space to give us a reliable weekly harvest instead of a once-a-year bulk crop that is weather dependent and exposed to the elements, predators, and pests.

When it comes to measuring the yield of other systems, we must quantify the number of plants you can grow, not the weight of the product. Because every system, plant, fish, and grower is different, it is not reasonable to suggest that everyone should expect the same weight and quality of yield. What I can be certain of is the capability of a system to produce a certain quantity of plants for each crop type under ideal operating conditions.

Chapter 5 (see page 59) guides you through building six different systems. The following tables provide a preview of what plant quantities to expect relative to your fish stocking density, crop type, and grow bed style used. Leafy greens generally fall under the 6-week crop category, with all other herbs, fruits, and vegetables in the 12-week category.

100-Square-Foot - Annual Plant Count Estimate @ Stock Density

Grow Bed	Qty	SqFt	Gals	Plant Sites	6-Week Crops				12-Week Crops			
Fish	-	-	50*	-	Plants/Week	17	10	6	Plants/Week	17	10	6
Dutch	8	8	40	16	3	139	87	52	1	69	43	26
Media	1	8	40	24	4	208	130	78	2	104	65	39
Wicking	1	40	160	96	16	832	520	312	8	416	260	156
NFT	10	20	10	100	17	867	542	325	8	433	271	163
Towers	10	30	10	100	17	867	542	325	8	433	271	163
DWC	1	32	175	112	19	971	607	364	9	485	303	182

*50 gallons of water is the recommended size for a 100-square-foot area.

100-Square-Foot System - Plants / Year @ # Fish

# Fish*				6	10	17	6	10	17	6	10	17	6	10	17
Grow Bed	Qty	Sqft	Gal	Leafy @ 6 wk			Herbs @ 12 wk			Fruit @ 12 wk			Root @ 12 wk		
Media	1	8	40	78	130	208	39	65	104	39	65	104	39	65	104
Wicking	1	32	160	312	520	832	156	260	416	156	260	416	156	260	416
DWC	1	40	175	364	607	971	182	303	485	182	303	485	182	303	485
NFT	10	20	10	325	542	867	163	271	433	163	271	433	163	271	433
Towers	10	30	10	325	542	867	163	271	433	163	271	433	163	271	433
Dutch	8	8	40	26	43	69	52	87	139	52	87	139	52	87	139

*Gallons of water per fish in a 100-square-foot area: 6 fish have 8 gallons of water per fish, 10 fish have 5 gallons of water per fish, and 17 fish have 3 gallons of water per fish.

CHAPTER TWO

Before You Get Started

Building your own aquaponic system is a multidisciplinary feat, so I want you to have the knowledge and tools to do it right the first time. With attention to detail, appropriate safety measures, and some good ol' elbow grease, you can get it done and begin growing your own food.

This chapter breaks down the steps for selecting the best system for the plants you wish to grow. You'll gain advice on which fish and plants to consider growing together, and you'll learn about the important role of cultivating beneficial bacteria and incorporating worms. We will also discuss how to interpret water quality tests and what steps to take for adjusting water-chemistry values to reach media-bed target ranges, a crucial step in ensuring all organisms in your system are happy and healthy.

Key Terms

- Ammonia (NH_3)
- Calcium (Ca)
- Chelated iron (Fe)
- Cold-water system
- Dissolved oxygen (DO)
- Electrical conductivity (EC)
- Fruiting plants
- Herbs
- Leafy greens
- Mycorrhizae fungi
- Nitrate (NO_3)
- Nitrite (NO_2)
- Nutrient solution
- Parts per million (ppm)
- Pet fish
- pH
- Potassium (K)
- Priming
- Root crops
- Temperature
- Warm-water system

Picking the Best Aquaponic System

The best aquaponic system is one designed in a style that can grow the crops you want. With a diverse range of grow beds to choose from, it is important to know that not every system can grow every plant type well. Research conducted by both home gardeners and private companies proves that different crops do better in different grow beds. But how do you know which grow bed is right for your crops? We will discuss this as I introduce you to each grow bed and its corresponding pros and cons. Later, we will get into the steps for building each.

Some grow bed styles are capable of growing only a few crop types, while others can grow many. Other common traits are operational in nature, such as increased evaporation or modular parts that make it easy to modify, replace, or expand the system. As with any decision, it is a good idea to weigh the prominent pros and cons before making your choice.

System	Pros	Cons
Media	Grows most crops easily	Anaerobic zones
DWC	Ease of use for leafy greens	Algae growth common
Wicking	Grows root crops well	Lower oxygen content
NFT	Easy to modify and replace	High evaporation rates
Dutch	Great for fruit bushes and vines	Limited crop types
Vertical	Most plants per square foot	Most expensive option

In the world of aquaponics, grow beds can be large, small, long, or tall; it all depends on what you are growing. NFT channels and towers measure a few inches wide and can be held in your hands, while media and wicking beds measure many square feet and are very heavy. A simple lumber planter frame commonly used in gardening can be turned into a variety of grow beds just by changing its contents. Turnkey systems vary just as much as custom ones, only they have fewer steps for installation. Chapter 5 (see page 59) guides you through building a template system for each type of grow bed that is tailored to fit the same fish tank in a given space.

You can turn a single garden planter into one of three grow bed styles. Media beds use porous stones to hold plant roots in place. You can choose from a few types of media, but this style is capable of growing most types of plants. Wicking beds use layers of soil and porous stone to raise root crops. A wicking effect can be created in a media bed by using fabric pots of organic soil nestled in between the media to create what is called a dual root zone. Deep water culture (DWC) uses modular floating rafts with dozens of cells for plants. Optimal for leafy greens and select herbs, this method uses dense production that rotates from one end of the grow bed to the other.

With modular systems, aquapons get to use many small grow beds instead of a few large ones. Nutrient film technique (NFT) uses 10-foot-long channels of pipe or gutter with the flowing water method used in DWC to grow **leafy greens**, **herbs**, and select berries. Vertical towers resemble NFT channels, but they are shorter and stand upright, either on a wall or over a basin. Dutch buckets are small basins with media and a constant water exchange, and they are renowned for growing **fruiting plants** (vines and bushes) exceptionally well.

The location of your system—outdoors, indoors, or in a greenhouse—will impact production. Placing a system outdoors won't cost anything extra, but you will need to account for the unpredictability of nature and the elements. Installing a greenhouse can cost just as much as an indoor system if not more, but this can extend the growing season by many weeks. An indoor system gives you complete control over the growing environment, which is great if you can afford it. The space you have available will be the determining factor with regards to location. When setting up a large indoor system, it is always recommended to install the system on a concrete slab due to weight load concerns. Also, it is worth checking your homeowners insurance policy on water damage, as every company and policy is different.

I have created a table to help you narrow down the right system for you based on how much space you have, your budget, what you want to grow, and where you want to grow it. The Low Cost and High Cost columns multiply your square feet by an expense estimate of how much you will probably spend on materials for a DIY system to fit the space. The Turnkey Cost column does the same, but for prefabricated systems bought from a manufacturer.

System Expense Estimate				
	System Area	**Low Cost**	**High Cost**	**Turnkey Cost**
Questions to Get Started	Square feet	×$20	×$40	×$100
How many square feet are set aside for the system?				
What is your total budget for an aquaponic system?				
Which price point does your budget match?				
What type of plants do you want to grow?	**Leafy Greens**	**Herbs / Flowers**	**Fruiting Crops**	**Root Crops**
Most Successful Methods	DWC	Media	Media	Wicking
	NFT	Wicking	Dutch bucket	Dutch bucket
	Tower	Tower	Tower	Media
Where will your system be located?	**Pros**		**Cons**	
Outdoors	Plentiful sunlight	Helps native pollinators	Temperature changes	Susceptible to pests
Greenhouse	Plentiful sunlight	Season extension	Structure expenses	Cost to heat in winter
Indoors	Control over environment	Control over pests	Risk of mold from moisture	Environment control costs

Keep these considerations in mind when we delve into building your system in chapter 4 (see page 43). Many of the same tools and equipment are used to construct and install each system. There is an emphasis on adapting designs to structures, so while you let these tidbits sink in, let's get into the fish and plants you may want to grow together in your ideal system.

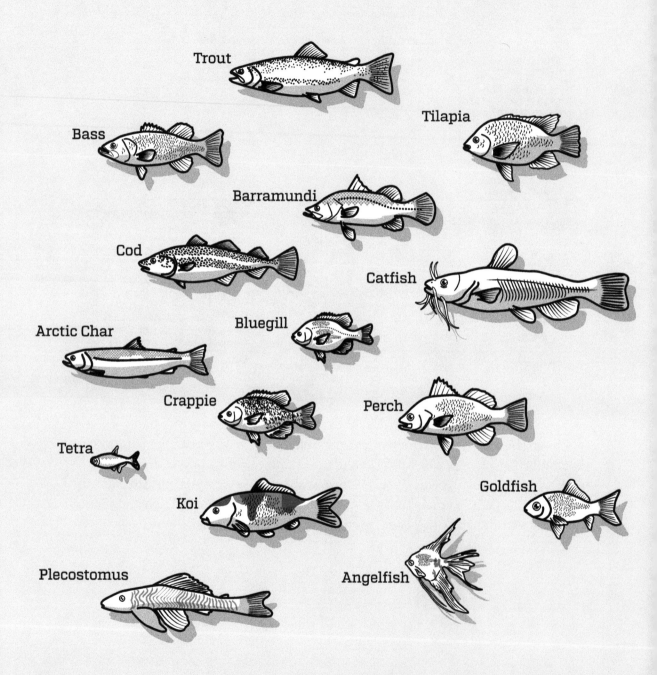

Trout

Tilapia

Bass

Barramundi

Cod

Catfish

Arctic Char

Bluegill

Crappie

Perch

Tetra

Goldfish

Koi

Plecostomus

Angelfish

Which Are the Best Fish to Raise?

The best fish for your aquaponic system depends on your intention and budget. That is the simplest answer. In terms of intention, you may want to grow fish for consumption, or you may want to treat them humanely as treasured pets that are appreciated for fertilizing your plants. The type of plants you want to grow also factors in, as some plants and fish thrive in cold water while others thrive in warm water. I have created a table to help you understand what fish and plants grow well in the same **temperature** ranges. This table introduces types of fish, how many months it takes for them to grow to one pound, and what plants go best with each.

Best Fish			
Cold		Warm	
55°F to 70°F		70°F to 85°F	
Breed	Month/Lb	Breed	Month/Lb
Arctic Char	12	Tilapia	9
Bass	12	Perch	12
Cod	18	Bluegill	12
Trout	18	Barramundi	12
Crappie	24	Catfish	18

For the pescatarians (fish eaters) out there, you probably want to grow some edible fish. In **warm-water systems**, those with 70°F to 85°F water, the most common fish are tilapia, catfish, and most perch species. These fish have faster metabolisms due to being raised in warm water. This correlates to faster growth rates: It only takes 9 to 12 months for the fish to reach a plate size of at least one pound. Be aware that warm water holds less oxygen, so you will have to pay for running water heaters and extra air pumps to raise these fish.

In **cold-water systems**, those with 55°F to 70°F water, edible fish such as trout, cod, or bass are most successful. Water warmer than 70°F may cause appetite loss. Colder water correlates to slower metabolisms, so expect your fish to gain a pound of protein over the course of 12 to 24 months. Salmon are not recommended for systems under 500 gallons because they become very large, are prone to disease, and grow slowly.

If **pet fish** are more your style, then the sky's the limit with selection. Anything from bluegill to tetras, angelfish, and koi will do. Some fish, like the redear sunfish, are known for consuming insects and snails that may make their way into the system, which makes them extra beneficial. Pet fish are also referred to as "ornamental," and they can sometimes be very expensive to acquire.

Many folks resort to goldfish or koi due to their availability, temperature adaptability, **pH** tolerance, and appetites. Goldies, the most iconic fish in the pet fish industry, are recognizable the world over and can be found at any pet store. In reality, any fish will do as long as you care for them properly, which means maintaining optimal water quality with proper filtration and following a regular feeding schedule.

Did you know that permits or licenses from government agencies are required to grow some fish in captivity? This is one of the few reasons that I highly recommend growing fish native to your part of the world. First of all, this ensures no invasive species will be released if a flood were to wash your facility away. Second, this precaution provides you with fish that not only are adapted to the climate and weather fluctuations, but also have evolved immune responses to native pathogens.

Which Are the Best Plants to Grow?

While you can attempt to grow any plant in a particular grow bed, there are pairings that produce higher yields than others (refer back to the table on page 15). For example, leafy greens perform best in deep water culture (DWC) beds, nutrient film technique (NFT) channels, or vertical towers. Herbs grow best in media beds, wicking beds, and towers. Fruiting vines and bushes grow best in Dutch buckets, media beds, and towers. Root crops are really only viable in wicking beds or Dutch buckets outfitted as mini wicking beds.

Let's take a closer look at the four basic categories of plants you may choose to grow.

Leafy greens

This covers a broad category of plants: basically anything you can build a salad from, such as lettuces, kales, collards, chard, escarole, endives, and the list goes on. There are thousands of varieties, each with nuanced nutrient requirements, ideal pH values, and growth time frames. Try to select at least three different plant types so as to reduce the odds of any infestations destroying your entire crop (see chapter 6, page 111). Planning for leafy greens means partitioning your grow space like we discussed in the example in chapter 1 (see page 7). Separate your rafts, towers, or channels to represent different weeks of transplants so you can have a reliable weekly harvest. Most leafy greens require far fewer nutrients than other crop types, which means they should be grown in a system with crops of like needs. While lettuces will be a full harvest plant (meaning you harvest the entire plant at once), others, like kale and collards, can be partial, which means you can harvest mature leaves as the plant continues to grow.

Best Plants					
Cold			**Warm**		
55°F to 70°F			70°F to 85°F		
Type	**Plant**		**Type**	**Plant**	
Leafy Greens	Lettuce		Leafy Greens	Pak choi	
	Mustard			Escarole	
	Kale			Collards	
Herbs	Mint		Herbs	Parsley	
	Oregano			Basil	
	Cilantro			Chives	
Fruits	Blueberry		Fruits	Peppers	
	Raspberry			Strawberry	
	Tomato			Tomato	
Roots	Potato		Roots	Sweet potato	
	Radish			Cassava	
	Carrot			Taro	

Herbs

Herbs are aromatic plants you can use to flavor your meals, and there are dozens of varieties to choose from. In an aquaponic system, herbs need some type of media to hold on to. Media and wicking beds provide porous stones and coir, moss, or soil. Towers typically use media net cups to hold herbs in place, while some manufacturers use patented recycled poly-media that performs exceptionally well. Typically requiring a medium nutrient density in the water for 10 to 12 weeks, herbs are generally partial harvest plants.

Fruiting plants

Fruiting plants such as berry bushes, peppers, tomatoes, and squashes provide great flavor and texture to meals. Fruits absolutely love Dutch bucket systems because they provide separation from other plants' root zones and provide vertical space to grow and expand. In a media bed, the fruit roots can get entangled and create anaerobic zones that result in occasional overflows, since the roots can impede the flow of water like a dam. Dutch buckets provide modularity that allows individual plants to be easily moved if they need more space without disturbing their roots.

Root crops

Root crops love compression, which is why wicking beds were created to mimic soil environments. Wicking beds provide many advantages over media beds, including that they do not require the optional siphons to flood and drain the grow bed. Instead, moisture wicks upward, saturating the lightweight media, and giving the root or tuber the compression it desires while still providing oxygen-rich water and nutrients. When grown in media beds, root crops can become deformed and succumb to rot.

Using Bacteria and Worms

Inoculating aquaponic systems with beneficial bacteria and symbiotic fungi like mycorrhizae creates a microbiome suitable to producing increased yields when compared to all other growing methods. The longer your system runs under regular maintenance, the stronger those beneficial bacteria colonies become. Soluble **mycorrhizae fungi** transport nutrients and minerals between root systems like a nutrient highway. On average, the inclusion of these microorganisms increases yields and nutrition values 10 to 20 percent in aquaponically grown produce.

Essential nitrifying bacteria convert **ammonia (NH_3)** from fish urine into bioavailable forms of nitrogen for your plants to consume. During the system cycling period (the first three to four weeks), these microorganisms are introduced and grown to digest liquid waste in the water and to colonize grow media by living on the porous biological surface area. After six months of ideal operating conditions, one bottle dosed during cycling can grow to colonize entire grow beds, speeding up nutrient conversion and helping plants grow faster.

Nitrifying bacteria are cultured in liquid. You can usually purchase them by the bottle in your local pet store's aquarium section or garden store's pond section. They require a minimum temperature of 55°F in order to metabolize their food. Otherwise they will go dormant and only reactivate at the right temperature within a given time window. Wait too long to bring that temperature up, and you will need to dose your system once more. Without these bacteria, the fish waste would build up to toxic levels that would kill your plants and fish alike. Recording water-chemistry measurements can give you insight as to the strength of your bacterial colonies and may provide indicators that adjustments need to be made.

As mentioned in chapter 1, aquaponic vermicompost is superior to normal compost in almost all regards (see page 2). It boasts twice the **calcium (Ca)**, and many times more nitrogen, **potassium (K)**, and phosphorus. As the water flows in a media bed, these worm castings dissolve into the water and provide plants with more bioavailable nutrients and minerals. In the aquaponic industry, we often refer to the nutrient-rich water as a **nutrient solution**, which is a term carried over from hydroponics.

After you fill your system with water but before you introduce fish and plants, you will add bacteria and worms so they can work their magic. This is known as **priming**, and it's a crucial step when setting up any aquaponic system. We'll go more into detail about priming in chapter 4 (see page 43). This process provides microbe food for these beneficial microorganisms to consume as they begin to colonize your media in preparation for the introduction of fish. This way they will be ready when that time comes so your system won't get overloaded with ammonia and crash.

Managing Water Purity, Temperature, and pH

Water purity is critical to a successful aquaponic system because it creates optimal conditions for your fish, plants, and microorganisms to all thrive. Priming with bacteria and worms sets the stage for fish to be introduced safely. Monitoring water quality measures, such as temperature, pH, and nitrogen, is key over the first three to four weeks to ensuring the best operating conditions for the organisms you choose to raise. This process (see chapter 4, page 55) only takes about five minutes each day to complete. As long as you stick to this water-chemistry routine, there should be few (if any) hiccups on your aquaponic journey.

Parameters

Both pH and **electrical conductivity (EC)** can be measured with handy and affordable wand meters that range in price from $20 to $200. Your pH measures for potential hydrogen in a solution. This determines the availability of nutrients to your plants. The aquaponics sweet spot is 6.5 to 6.8, a level that allows for nutrient uptake of all essential macro- and micronutrients while keeping fish happy. To increase pH, add carbonates; to lower it, add acids.

Rarely will a system need to have its pH lowered, and this is where chemistry can get complicated. This usually happens because of something inside

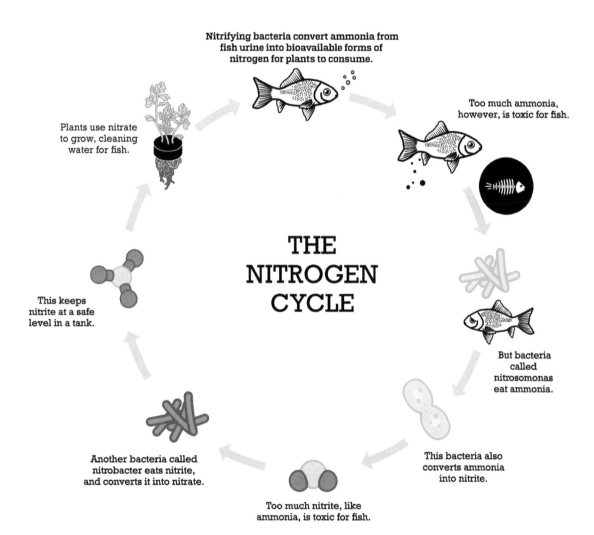

Nitrifying bacteria convert ammonia from fish urine into bioavailable forms of nitrogen for plants to consume.

Too much ammonia, however, is toxic for fish.

Plants use nitrate to grow, cleaning water for fish.

THE NITROGEN CYCLE

This keeps nitrite at a safe level in a tank.

But bacteria called nitrosomonas eat ammonia.

Another bacteria called nitrobacter eats nitrite, and converts it into nitrate.

This bacteria also converts ammonia into nitrite.

Too much nitrite, like ammonia, is toxic for fish.

your system, and that culprit is almost always media. If you must make the risky decision of dosing phosphoric acid or muriatic acid into your system (which can easily kill your fish and bacteria), give those pH-lowering agents a few days to work. Read the directions closely, as concentrations vary, and always dose a little bit at a time, with days between applications. As you will come to find out, doing your research on products, plants, and fish will help you plan for success.

Electrical conductivity (EC) measures the concentration of dissolved salts (nutrients) in your water. The target level of EC depends on the plants you grow: Leafy greens require low values, herbs require values in the mid-range, and fruits or vegetables require the most. To increase the EC value, add fish or increase feed rates; to decrease EC, remove fish or lower feed rates.

Temperature is regulated by using water heater probes that can be set to a target temperature. On average, these take 1 watt of electricity to heat 1 gallon of water 1°F over an hour. In a medium-size system of 250 gallons, a 250-watt heater will take 10 hours to raise the water's temperature from 50°F to 60°F before clicking off and on to maintain that temperature. Recall that the proper temperature for your tanks depends on both the fish and plants you cultivate, as different fish and plants thrive in cold and warm systems (see pages 17 and 20).

Dissolved oxygen (DO) measures the **parts per million (ppm)** of oxygen in the water and is an optional parameter to keep track of, since DO meters easily cost from a few hundred to a thousand dollars. Oxygen is normally added with air pumps that are associated with the quarter-inch tubing that connects the pump to air stones. These porous stones are submerged and emit microbubbles when resting on the bottom of a tank or grow bed, so as long as you have those in play, you should be fine. Your target DO level should be a minimum of 5 ppm. Locations for air stones are fish tanks, sump tanks, DWC beds, biofilters, and remineralization tanks. Make sure your air pump sits at a higher elevation than the water table it is supplying with air. For sizing an air pump, refer to chapter 4 (see page 48).

Nutrients

Just as we prefer to consume nutrient-rich foods, plants like to consume nutrient-rich water. The nutrients plants consume come in the form of salts that are dissolved into the water forming a nutrient solution. Macronutrients are a category of elements that plants need large amounts of, while micronutrients and trace minerals are needed in much smaller quantities. In this section you will learn about the primary macronutrients, as they are the most important.

Nitrogen plays a key role in aquaponics, and as an aquapon, you'll monitor three versions. Most practitioners use ink dropper test kits that add a few drops of dye to water samples in order to discover their nitrogen values. The first is ammonia (NH_3), which is excreted mostly as liquid waste from your fish, and to some extent solids, too. A good target range for ammonia is 1 to 2 ppm. Any higher can create toxicity in your fish that first shows as black ammonia burns on the tips of their fins. To reduce NH_3, either add bacteria if they are not present or reduce feed rates.

Nitrite (NO_2) results when *Nitrosomonas* bacteria convert ammonia into nitrite. Toxic even at low concentrations, do your best to ensure this stays below 1 ppm, which it will rarely go over. If nitrite does go over 1 ppm during regular operations, add bacteria. In rare occasions that nitrite measures over 2 ppm, you may want to consider quarantining your fish until you can bring that level under 1 ppm.

Nitrobacter bacteria adds an extra oxygen particle to nitrite, creating the plant food **nitrate (NO_3)**. This is our end result, and we aim for systems to have between 20 to 60 ppm for ideal feeding levels. If you have low levels, increase feeding rates. If you have no nitrates or nitrites, but you do detect ammonia present, add beneficial bacteria. If nitrate levels are over 60 ppm, reduce feed rates.

Calcium (Ca) and potassium (K) share the same cell receptors and can be detected through the same ink dropper tests. It is recommended to amend your system water by taking turns and rotating, adding the organic amendments calcium carbonate one week and potassium bicarbonate the next. With varying potency between products, read the directions and add each dose to a cup or pitcher of system water until it is dissolved before pouring it into your sump tank or grow bed water. Another calcium alternative is using hydrated lime in low doses the same way. These will raise and buffer the pH to keep it stable over time, so be patient and retest pH a few hours after dosing.

The following nutrients are easier to observe as deficiencies than to detect, since the cost of equipment is very high. For that reason, we preemptively implement regular dosing in our maintenance routine. Epsom salt provides enough magnesium and sulfur in relatively low dosages of 1 teaspoon per 100 gallons once a month. A **chelated iron (Fe)** considered food grade of either EDTA (for pH up to 6.5) or DTPA (up to pH of 7.5) at half a tablespoon per 100 gallons once a month will provide enough iron for most crops. Simply dissolve it in system water the same way as other amendments. All other trace minerals can be supplemented with rock dust or liquid seaweed dosed at 1 tablespoon per 100 gallons once a month.

CHAPTER THREE

Planning Your First System

Now that you know the basics of how to run a system, it is time to create an **action plan**: the strategy to accomplish your goal. Research further into what plants you want to grow, which style bed they grow best in, and what type of fish you want. As long as you incorporate biomimicry into your design, you will have success. To help you out, this chapter walks you through an ideal planning process so that you will have the necessary skills to manage your garden successfully.

Following through with a regular maintenance routine is imperative to giving your household food sovereignty. You are about to learn key tenets of how to make daily maintenance simple and easy, including the order of processes, how to set up an ideal calendar, and how to map out your system. It all begins with research and planning, so let's get into it!

Key Terms

- ◆ Action plan
- ◆ SMART goals
- ◆ Yield mapping

Creating an Action Plan for Your Systems

Creating an action plan is critical to following through on your project, whether it be for a home garden system or a farm business model. Action plans are road maps used to set realistic goals that create a viable path to milestones, which signal big achievements along the way to reaching your end goal. It's all about taking those simple baby steps to complete your big-picture mission.

Up to this point, you have learned how to select a system based on what you want to grow, your budget, and available space. I've introduced you to how these systems work, their advantages over other growing methods, and what you can reasonably expect. The level of success you have is intimately related to how well you keep up with a maintenance routine and how well you tailor your system to your crops through planning and research.

Close your eyes and envision an ideal aquaponic system in your home. See it in the space you have set aside, breathe in the oxygen coming off the plants, hear the tranquil trickling of water, and taste the bounty that comes out of your harvests. Now use this simple checklist to help you brainstorm your specific goals. Write your thoughts on a blank sheet of paper.

Action Plan Brainstorm Checklist

- ☐ Why are you farming with aquaponics?
- ☐ Which crops and fish will you harvest?
- ☐ What is your long-term goal for growing with aquaponics?
- ☐ Are you using aquaponics to become more self-reliant?
- ☐ Do you want to set up a side business with aquaponics?

Answering these questions will provide insight into the steps you need to take. After you brainstorm, you can reorganize your thoughts and goals into a time line. Once you have your goals in mind, use the chapters in this book to help you select, build, and maintain a system. After you fill up and cycle your system, you will need to anticipate when to expect your first harvests. Here are some more questions to help you brainstorm short-term year-one goals.

Year-One Goals Brainstorm Checklist

- ☐ How long until your first plant harvest?
- ☐ How long until your first fish harvest?
- ☐ Will you be able to use all the parts of the plants you grow to reduce waste?

- ☐ Have you considered sharing extra with your neighbors or community?
- ☐ When will you review your system plan and reassess what you want to grow? Six months? One year?

Most systems are able to grow enough food over the course of a year to pay for the investment put into building them. For example, the 24-square-foot lettuce raft system mentioned in chapter 1 could produce 600 heads in a year (see page 8). Sold at $3, each gives us an $1,800 production value. With a per-square-foot cost of $20 to $40, we could afford a 45- to 90-square-foot system, which would give us enough space to grow and navigate. This means we could grow enough lettuce in that system in 12 months' time to recover the expense taken to build the system.

I highly recommend that you take the time to review your first year and compare your results to your projections. Did your routine measure up to your expectations? If so, then you may want to consider expanding your system, or even starting a small farm business. No matter your results, when resetting your goals, make sure to keep them realistic.

Keeping Your Goals Realistic

It is easy to get caught up in the possibilities of what these systems can do, so make sure to check yourself before you get carried away. Once most people have that light-bulb moment about how productive aquaponic systems can potentially be, the fire is lit and it can be hard to dial back that flame. While aquaponic systems often do turn most crops into high-yielding nutritious bounties, they are not able to do so without a regular maintenance routine that keeps everything in the system happy and in homeostasis. Tending your aquaponic garden on a daily or weekly basis involves money to pay for inputs (fish feed, water, and electricity).

If you have big dreams and a lower-than-ideal bank-account balance, don't give up—I sure didn't. Starting small with a decent tabletop turnkey system for a few hundred bucks can help you get your bearings and decide if aquaponics is right for you without getting too invested. If you are a tad more ambitious, have the passion, and know you will want to expand your system when you can afford it, then plan your design to accommodate that desire.

A common tool used in project management is the concept of **SMART goals**. SMART is an acronym for **S**pecific, **M**easurable, **A**ttainable, **R**ealistic, and **T**imely, all characteristics of effective goals. Answer the questions in the table on pages 34 to 35 to discover how you can develop and set SMART goals to stay on track with your aquaponic project.

SMART Goals for Your Aquaponic System

	Specific	Answers
S	What do you want to accomplish?	
	Why is that goal important to you?	
	Who will be involved?	
	Where will your system go?	
	When will it be installed?	

	Measurable	Answers
M	What do the materials cost?	
	How long will it take to install?	
	How much is a permit (if applicable)?	
	How will you maintain the system?	
	How much time will you need each week for maintenance?	

	Attainable	Answers
A	Have you raised plants before?	
	Have you raised fish before?	
	Can you use power tools safely?	
	Should you take some classes?	
	Would you hire a professional?	

	Realistic	Answers
R	How confident are you?	
	Do you have all the tools?	
	Do you have the time for maintenance?	
	What could you learn more about?	
	What is one short-term goal you can set?	

	Timely	Answers
T	When can you begin research?	
	When would you like your system built?	
	Do you have a system calendar?	
	What would be a good first harvest date?	
	How long will your inputs last?	

Let's go back to our DWC lettuce example (see page 8) to see how SMART can help set goals for that system.

Specific. I want to grow 12 heads of lettuce every week indoors under a grow light in my DWC bed because I want to eat two salads every day.

Measurable. My DWC system won't need a permit and will cost around $1,800 to build over two days. I'll spend one hour every week analyzing the plants to keep them on track and healthy.

Attainable. I have completed professional aquaponic training courses, worked with systems for years, and have experience with power tools.

Realistic. While I have all the tools to build it and time to maintain it, perhaps I could ask the people I want to sell lettuce to which variety they would like to buy. Then I can research the specific needs for that variety of lettuce, such as pH, temperature, and nutrient preferences.

Timely. I can begin market and plant variety research this week, apply that knowledge to my action plan, and build a system next week that will give me my first harvest 11 weeks from today. From here, I would apply my results to a calendar so I could follow a preplanned trajectory for success.

In addition to SMART goals, you should consider contingency plans for anything that could go wrong in your system. Natural disasters such as earthquakes, floods, tornados, and hurricanes can interrupt growth cycles and destroy property, so insuring your system may be a good idea if you live in places prone to such events. Some more common situations and their solutions include:

A dead air pump or a power outage kills your fish. You can keep bottled ammonia on hand to replace the fish waste so you can keep your bacteria and plants alive while you source new fish. An alternative would be to have organic hydroponic nutrients ready to use in case you run out of ammonia.

You must drain all the water from your system. It's unlikely that you would need to do this, but just in case, you can plan for it when you design your system, choosing to connect all of your plumbing together with ball valves that are closed during operation but can be opened to drain everything out.

An air or water pump breaks. Have extra equipment on hand so you can replace them if they ever falter or die.

An exterminator tents your neighbor's house, and the gases waft over to your outdoor system, killing your fish, bacteria, and eventually your plants. This situation is a good opportunity for a preemptive contingency measure where you tell your neighbor that you will be installing an aquaponic garden outside and ask them to notify you ahead of time if they ever need to have their house tented.

Setting Up an Aquaponic Calendar

Calendars and schedules are an important part of traditional gardening and farming. Although aquaponic systems function outside the bounds of seasonal weather, it's still important for aquapons to stick to regular operations and maintenance schedules, which we explore in detail in chapter 6 (see page 111).

In the meantime, let's review some key concepts for when it comes to planning an operations calendar. There are tasks you should do every day, once a week, and once a month in order to maintain a healthy system. Without these, the risk of system imbalances increases, and imbalances can throw off your planned schedule. The following tables introduce basic task schedules. Refer to the checklists at the end of the book (see page 134) that expand upon these tables.

Daily Tasks for an Aquaponic System		
Equipment Check	**Grow Area Walk-Through**	**Fish and Water**
☐ Wash your hands	☐ Wash your hands	☐ Wash your hands
☐ Check filters for flow	☐ Noticeable deficiencies?	☐ Feed fish
☐ Equipment plugged in?	☐ Pest incidence?	☐ Secure feed
☐ Air stones bubbling?	☐ Under-leaf checks	☐ Gill check
☐ Timers calibrated?	☐ Puddles?	☐ Behavior check
☐ Lights functioning?	☐ Trim overgrowth	☐ Check water chem
☐ Wash your hands	☐ Wash your hands	☐ Wash your hands

Weekly Tasks		Monthly Tasks
Grow Area Walk-Through	**Fish and Water**	**General**
☐ Daily tasks	☐ Daily tasks	☐ Daily tasks
☐ Harvest	☐ Quarantine needed?	☐ Weekly tasks
☐ Transplant	☐ Solids extraction	☐ Compile data
☐ Sow seeds	☐ Top off water	☐ Iron dosing
☐ Pest controls	☐ Carbonate dosing	☐ Measure fish

If you can stick to that baseline operating calendar, you should have no problem with aquaponics. As long as you do proper research to plan for the unexpected, nothing will be a surprise, and your contingency plans will address any pest, leak, or other mishap. It always helps to map your system out in a manner that works well with your routine.

Mapping Out Your Systems

Mapping out your system refers to both physical and statistical means. Organizing the layout of which components will go where within the space is a very important step in the design process once you know what grow beds you will be using. After your system is installed, it behooves you to keep records as detailed as possible so you can map the progress, efficiency, and yields of your system.

Once you know where you want your aquaponic system, measure the length, width, and height of the space. When we estimate ballpark figures for systems, we use spatial dimensions as the key. As an example, let's use a 10 × 10 × 8-foot space, which gives us a 100-square-foot area. On average, about 50 percent of that space can be used to host grow beds. Fish tanks and filters take up about 20 percent. The remaining 30 percent of space is for walk paths and storage.

Depending on the variety of system you choose, there will be additional considerations. For vertical systems, the eight-foot height means you probably won't be able to have a tower taller than five feet on the wall, or six feet standing solo. You need to leave space below the bottom of the tower for either a fish tank or collection basin, and room above the tower for plants to grow vertically.

For a hybrid system, you need access to grow beds at waist height, between three and four feet. This creates space not only below the beds for water to be collected but also for vertical room that allows plants to grow upward. If you intend on using grow lights, let them hang at least a foot down from the ceiling to allow for airflow to cool them off and so they can broadcast their light over the proper area. This provides your plants with a three- to four-foot vertical space for them to grow before touching the light source.

When factoring gravity into the equation, remember that a body of water will always seek to level between two containers. Grow beds early in the flowchart will be at higher elevations than those farther along in the flow due to the water tables being at lower elevations with each successive grow bed. This essential design practice ensures overflows are very unlikely to happen and that troubleshooting issues will be relatively straightforward.

Aside from mapping out the physical specs of your system, you should also map out your system's yields. **Yield mapping** is the process of comparing results across harvests and time. Even in the planning phase, you can estimate how long plants will take to germinate, establish roots for transplanting, and grow to harvest. From research, you may be able to find potential yields for each specific variety of plant you intend to grow. During your internal audits, you will review your recorded results and compare them to your expectations in order to map your yields.

Over that time, ask yourself what quantity of inputs you need to grow your plants. These may include fish feed, water amendments, and electricity for pumps and lights. Measuring your final products' harvest weight, size, and health is also key. Armed with those variables, you can discover valuable data to track the cost efficiency, growth rates, and the benefits of different feeding or lighting schedules.

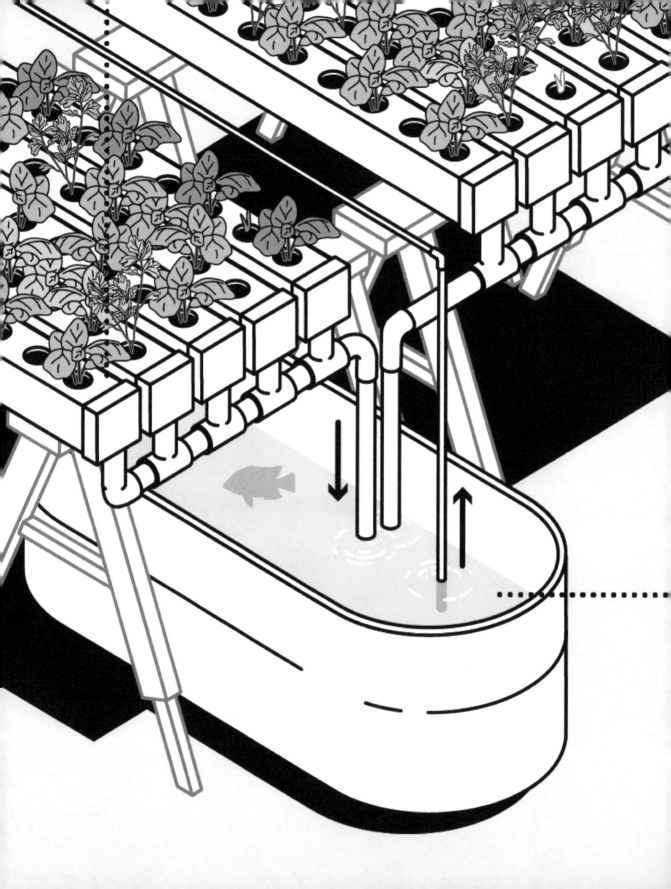

CHAPTER FOUR

Building Your First System

Going from built to bounty isn't an overnight process: It takes time and care. We all want our first system to serve as a pivotal point in our journey that marks when we began successfully growing our own food. After learning from my own mistakes as well as those of my mentors and clients, I've uncovered the most common errors when it comes to aquaponics, along with some incredibly simple solutions.

This chapter highlights critical components relative to all aquaponic system designs, walks you through the steps of preparing your fish tank, and introduces different types of filters recommended for these systems. Remember that all aquaponic systems require a grow bed for your plants, a tank for your fish, and your bacteria environment. We'll take a comprehensive look at how to arrange, start, prime, and cycle your system so that the organisms you introduce can thrive. Along the way, I'll offer solutions to common problems so that you are set up for success.

Key Terms

- Acrylonitrile butadiene styrene (ABS)
- Air pumps
- Analog timer
- Biological surface area (BSA)
- Bulkheads
- Coconut coir
- Cycling
- Digital timer
- Ethylene propylene diene monomer (EPDM)
- Fishless cycling
- Glass or acrylic aquariums
- Head height (HH)
- Heavyweight media
- High-density polyethylene (HDPE)
- Intermediate bulk container (IBC)
- Lava rock
- Lightweight expanded clay aggregate (LECA)
- Lightweight media
- Low-density polyethylene (LDPE)
- Moving bed biofilm reactor (MBBR)
- Peat moss
- Priming
- Radial filter
- Remineralization tank
- Schedule-40 PVC (polyvinyl-chloride)
- Smart plugs
- Specific surface area (SSA)
- Swirl filter
- Valves
- Water pump

Basic Hardware Components

The basic hardware shared by all systems is primarily related to raising fish and bacteria. Facilitating the fertilization and nutrient conversion process is the backbone of any successful aquaponic system, big or small. To simplify things, let's break the hardware down into three categories: grow beds and tanks (culturing containers), plumbing components, and growing media.

Grow Beds and Tanks

Grow beds and tanks are containers used to culture or raise organisms, whether they be fish, bacteria, worms, mushrooms, or plants. The DIY world is full of unique and resourceful options for culturing containers, but here we'll focus on the food-safe materials.

When people think about fish tanks, they automatically picture aquariums. If you have either **glass or acrylic aquariums** in mind, you can be successful with them. When selecting a tank, choose one with compartments that can house a pump, which will reduce the possibility of your fish meeting a messy demise. Aside from that, consider ways to protect the tank from sunlight exposure and algae growth. Either place the fish tank out of direct sunlight or make an enclosure to keep sunlight out. When using an aquarium, make sure you never rest anything on top of it, because in some cases the object's weight will cause the glass or acrylic to break.

For fish tanks larger than 50 gallons, **high-density polyethylene (HDPE)** comes into play as the dominant material. This food-safe plastic is melted down to create molded grow beds and fish tanks in many shapes and sizes. While very cheap as a raw material, aquaponic products made from HDPE are usually very expensive. When shopping for HDPE containers, look for those that are molded into the shape and size you need in black or blue, because these colors are UV resistant. Large HDPE fish tanks should be waist-high and round.

Filters made from HDPE should be tall, slim cylinders. Filters with conical bottoms allow solids to settle for easy extraction with a connected valve. The most common DIY option is to use an HDPE 55-gallon barrel and modify it into the filter you want to use. Some HDPE containers are shallow rectangles that serve as flood tables ideal for sprouting seeds or growing microgreens. This is the same material used to make square or round Dutch buckets.

An **intermediate bulk container (IBC)** tote is the most common choice of HDPE fish tank due to its low cost, large capacity of 250 gallons, and cubed shape. Grower beware! While fantastic as a fish tank, building your entire system out of IBC totes is not recommended for many reasons, including:

- The clear HDPE they're made of degrades from UV exposure and warps from heat.
- Their round edges force you to cut rafts to fit, compromising their integrity.
- The metal cages present hazards with sharp edges.
- They have limited volume as grow beds.
- They are at high risk for leaks due to multiple contact points.

Low-density polyethylene (LDPE) is a food-safe, flexible white film material with woven fibers inside to increase durability. In aquaponic systems, LDPE is used to line the insides of lumber-framed grow beds, which is often far cheaper and more aesthetically pleasing when compared to rigid HDPE molded beds. Staples and/or battens secure the liner in place.

Sourcing either material is best done online unless there is a hydroponics shop nearby. The only other places you may find HDPE containers in person will most likely be at a farm supply co-op or pond and landscape store. LDPE can only be purchased online in 6- or 12-foot-wide rolls under the trade name Dura-Skrim for $1 to $2 per square foot. There are multiple manufacturers and retailers who sell both products on their web stores, and even a few aquaponic companies that sell turnkey systems made from expensive HDPE materials.

Plumbing Components

Plumbing is an often overly complicated topic in aquaponics, but it doesn't have to be. Connecting tanks, filters, and grow beds together is done with food-safe pipe, fittings, and bulkheads. Water flows through the pipes, which are connected together by fittings that change the direction of the flow. The most common types of fittings are 90-degree elbows that shift the flow at right angles, couplings that connect straight pipes together, and tee fittings that connect two parallel pipes to a perpendicular one. The pipe and fitting configurations for every system are different, but they all serve the same purpose of continuing the flow without leaks between containers.

Bulkheads are plastic parts that connect system components to pipes so that water may flow between them without leaking. They are large threaded fittings that come with a rubber gasket and tightening nut. Each bulkhead with its gasket is placed in a predrilled hole from inside a fish tank, grow bed, or filter. From the outside the nut is spun onto the threads and wound as tight as it can go. This action squishes the gasket on the inside, creating a watertight seal. Silicone caulking is commonly applied to the gasket before insertion as a fail-safe to ensure the watertight seal stays that way.

Valves are another common plumbing component that controls the rate of flow between containers. There are many types of valves for different purposes. Ball valves have handles for manual opening and closing that are commonly used to either regulate water flow into grow beds or to drain solids out of filters. Gate valves resemble guillotines, and their primary purpose is to serve as an emergency drain valve if you ever have to empty your system.

Food-safe hydroponic and aquaponic systems almost exclusively use **schedule-40 PVC (polyvinyl-chloride)** for pipes and fittings because it is certified food safe. Schedule-40 is used for low-pressure water delivery, while sometimes schedule-80 (also food-safe) is used for high-pressure delivery. The only exceptions are for select **acrylonitrile butadiene styrene (ABS)** parts, such as bulkheads, and **ethylene propylene diene monomer (EPDM)** for thick black pond liner, gaskets, and uniseals. All three products are nontoxic and have a high UV tolerance.

Connecting pipe to a fitting is easy if you use the correct equipment. PVC cutters ratchet through most pipes two inches or less in diameter and are recommended instead of using a chop saw. Here's how to do it:

1. Using measuring tape, measure the distance of pipe needed, and be sure to account for the space inside the fittings.

2. Apply purple PVC primer to the outside end of the pipe and inside the fitting that are to be connected together.

3. After 30 seconds of drying time, apply clear PVC glue to both the primed sections.

4. While still wet, quickly connect the two glued pieces together, twist 90 degrees, and hold in place for another 30 seconds to set and cure.

5. Repeat as necessary for every PVC connection.

Water pumps raise water to a certain elevation and are easy to select if you know what you need. In general, you want to move the volume of your fish tank once an hour whether it's continuous or on a timer. The distance from your pump up to your highest grow bed is called the **head height (HH)**. Look for a pump that can move the volume of your fish tank once an hour at the head height you need. Check the GPH/HH graph, which shows how many gallons per hour the pump can move on the x-axis at the given HH on the y-axis. This graph is commonly found on your pump's box or documentation to find a match.

If you want to regulate your electricity usage, incorporating timers to set your water pump on a schedule is your best bet. **Analog timers** typically have a dial with tabs you can set to turn connected devices on or off in 15-minute intervals. **Digital timers** often are limited to the quantity of times you can set devices to turn off or on, but with greater accuracy down to the minute. If you aim for higher levels of automation, you may opt for an irrigation controller to control water pumps and solenoid valves that act as computer-triggered ball valves. **Smart plugs** connect your phone via Wi-Fi to your devices for highly customizable timer control of your pumps, lights, and more, which you can access remotely from wherever you travel.

Air pumps are crucial devices that provide oxygen to your beneficial bacteria, fish, and plant roots. They should match the size of your fish tank in gallons per hour (GPH). Many are rated in liters per hour, so multiply that number by 0.26 to find the GPH. Most commercial air pumps come with valve manifolds that provide air to multiple air stones via quarter-inch tubing that connects the two. The amount of quarter-inch tubing you need can be figured out by estimating the distance from the pump to each air stone location. Your air pump should remain on 24/7 and be stationed above the highest water table being supplied.

Growing Media

When using media beds or wicking beds, you will require one or two varieties of media to help things grow: lightweight media and heavyweight media. **Lightweight media** is used for propagation and seed sprouting. Soil, **coconut coir**, **peat moss**, fish-derived vermicompost, or a combination thereof are great examples of lightweight media for a sprout station or wicking bed. They are easy to work with, absorb water easily, and are either fibrous, grainy, or somewhere in between.

Heavyweight media is a type of substrate used in media beds for holding plants in place and culturing beneficial bacteria. Higher porosity allows water and air to permeate the media easily. This is because porous media has a high **specific surface area (SSA)**, which is expressed as square feet per cubic foot. As a rule of thumb, aquaponic systems require at least a one-to-one ratio of fish-tank water to media bed volume for adequate bacteria colonization using media with an SSA of 70 or higher. It also allows worms to hunt solid wastes and for plant roots to set anchor. Always rinse your media before adding it to your grow bed. **Biological surface area (BSA)** refers to the total SSA in your grow bed. For example, if you have 50 cubic feet of media with an SSA of 70 square feet per cubic foot, then you have a BSA of 3,500 square feet for bacteria to live on.

The best heavyweight media options for aquaponics are **lava rock** and **lightweight expanded clay aggregate (LECA)**, since they both have a high SSA, of about 70 square feet per cubic foot. The latter tends to be more expensive, but very easy to work with given its round quality that comes from being artificial. Commercially available under the name Hydroton, LECA is inert, so it won't alter the water chemistry. Crushed lava cinders and lava rock are commonly available in quarter- to half-inch sizes. Lava rock shares all the same properties as LECA, but it is naturally occurring. There are ample sources around the world, and it's an affordable alternative to LECA.

Crushed granite is also used as heavyweight media, but its SSA is a quarter that of LECA. While not porous, the quarter-inch size provides enough surface area for bacteria to colonize. If you choose crushed granite, you need four times as much as you would of LECA to provide enough BSA for proper nutrient conversion.

Lightweight media tend to be soft, and can retain water, but cannot dissolve into a solution. Examples of this type are often stringy and derived from natural sources. When used in an aquaponics environment, it is usually in either a wicking bed or in run-to-waste pots with drip irrigation. **Coconut coir** and **peat moss** are both preferred options with nearly identical properties. Coconut coir is the husk material from the outside of a coconut and is a sustainably sourced substrate. Peat moss, on the other hand, tends to be harvested from sensitive ecosystems called bogs that are nonrenewable.

Perlite is not advised, despite its common use in hydroponic systems. Perlite is volcanic rock that is heated to 900°C, making it sterile and lightweight with high porosity. Both this product and vermiculite are not recommended for aquaponic systems, as they are quite literally volcanic glass that shreds fish gills on contact, causing them to bleed out with no remedy.

General Steps for Starting an Aquaponic System

Most systems use the same equipment—fish tanks, filtration systems, and grow beds—in different arrangements to achieve different results. Just as vehicles will get you from point A to B, aquaponics will do the same. The style of the system must be tailored to what is being grown. However, there are some common basic steps to set any system up.

1. Install Your Fish Tank with AN SLO

For the most part, the fish provide the necessary fertilizer, so it's a good idea to install your fish tank first. No matter the format of your fish tank, you will need to use an SLO (see page 3). If you are using an aquarium, I recommend placing a sponge filter over the intake of your pump or buy a partitioning screen that creates a separate compartment for a pump. The goal here is to prevent fish from getting stuck to the pump and suffering the consequences.

For an IBC or other HDPE fish tank, the SLO should be centered with a central pipe that has holes or slices cut into the bottom to suck solid waste into the column of water that ascends the PVC and overflows through a bulkhead into either a media bed or a filter. At the top of the SLO pipe, a tee fitting will be connected to a perpendicular pipe that sends the solids water toward a bulkhead and out of the tank. The third side of the tee fitting that would host another vertical pipe is left open to the air, serving as a vent that prevents a vacuum from developing that would otherwise drain the fish tank of all its water.

2. Install a Filtration System

Filters come in many shapes and sizes, and their primary purpose is to extract solids. Small systems commonly use media beds as biofilters. Systems over 50 gallons in size should use some form of solids-extraction filter before the flow reaches any grow beds. **Swirl filters** and **radial filters** are the two most common styles of cylindrical-shaped filters that have solids-evacuation valves attached to the bottom for removing collected solids once a week. **Moving bed biofilm reactors (MBBR)** replace media beds as a beneficial bacteria colony for nutrient conversion. Let's take a closer look at each option.

Swirl filters send water in a circle, with solids sinking down the sides to the bottom. The key is to add a 90-degree elbow to your inlet that distributes the incoming water along the side of the barrel in a swirling motion. This draws solids to the side and downward. The outlet should be drilled a few inches below the inlet with the pipe extending to the center of the barrel, with a 90-degree angle facing upward on the end to catch the solid-free water.

Radial filter inlets enter from underneath the system, sending water up the center of the filter, where it meets a larger-diameter pipe encompassing the inlet. This directs solids to sink, with the column surrounding the bigger pipe containing the few solids that carry over to the next container via an overflow outlet near the top of the filter.

MBBR are often referred to simply as biofilters. A high-surface-area media like LECA or HDPE is aerated, causing the media to continuously be in motion. The bacteria present receive tons of oxygen from the aeration and ample nutrients in the form of dissolved solids. These are typically half the volume of the fish tank.

Remineralization tanks are an optional accessory that is disconnected from the main flow. Instead of having your solids filters drain from a spigot to a bucket for composting, you can instead have that valve direct solids into a remineralization tank. Beneficial bacteria are constantly aerated here, gradually converting those solids into bioavailable nutrients that are then reintroduced to the main flow.

3. Arrange Your Grow Beds

With filters in place, it's time to arrange the grow beds you've chosen accordingly (see chapter 5, page 59). Some systems will use grow beds that require media while others will not. Follow the guidelines set forth in each system's section. Once your grow beds are in place, move on to the sump tank.

4. Install Your Sump Tank

Set your sump tank (if applicable) in place near the fish tank. This should measure at least half the volume of your fish tank. The close proximity prevents large columns of water from applying unwanted pressure on your water pump, allowing a lower-wattage pump to be more effective. The water pump will be situated inside the sump tank and should always be completely submerged. If the water level decreases too much, the pump will not recirculate water and could overheat.

5. Install Plumbing

All bulkhead locations should set and cure for 24 hours before being used to connect plumbing. Plumbing should be installed after all system components are in place. Some people choose to dry-fit plumbing together without primer and glue first to test their system, and only then do they drain, disconnect all plumbing, and prime and glue everything together. Whether you choose that route or opt to go for the gold the first time, your glued pipes and fittings should sit for 24 hours to allow PVC glue to set and cure before adding water.

6. Add Water

When adding water, make sure you use an in-line hose water filter. This type of filter uses charcoal to filter out heavy metals and chlorine that would otherwise harm your beneficial bacteria. While the water filter will slow the fill rate, it will also ensure you are introducing good-quality water into your system. Always begin by filling the container with the highest water table first. This will ensure that the flow will move to containers with successively lower and lower water tables until reaching the lowest container. Once your lowest container is half full, turn off the hose and allow any water moving through the system to reach the end container. This may take a few minutes with a larger system.

Once water stops trickling into what will most likely be the sump, begin to fill this container directly until it is full. Write "Full" on the inside of the container at the water level with a permanent marker to dictate what level to refill this container to. Next, set a stopwatch and turn on the pump, then wait for the water evacuated from the sump to begin pouring back in after having traveled throughout the system. Once this happens, stop the clock to see how long it took and make a mark for "Low" at this water table level. This mark will serve as an indicator for you to fill it up or "top off" your system in the future if the water level reaches this point.

While you can add plants now, you will want to make sure the pH is adequate for them to grow healthily. To do this, there are some crucial steps you must take to prime the system, add bacteria, and reach an equilibrium of water-chemistry parameters to allow fish and plants to thrive.

General Steps for Aquaponic Cycling

Cycling your system is the imperative process of preparing it for fish and plants. This involves a particular order of events to set up the best possible scenario biologically for system success. It requires a month of patience and diligent testing, but it will pay off big in the end. Bacteria set the stage for balanced water chemistry that allows for easy introduction of fish and plants.

1. Aeration

As discussed in chapter 2 (see page 11), the use of air pumps is key to a functional system. Continuous oxygenation of the water creates an aerobic environment within the system that encourages the colonies of beneficial bacteria, fish, and plants to grow. Locations that receive air stones should be fish tanks, MBBR, float beds, the sump tank, and the remineralization tank if you choose to use one.

Remember that air pumps should always be stored at a higher elevation than the highest water table it is supplying with air. Each air pump should be able to supply multiple air stones with air, so small systems will need just one air pump, while larger systems may need two or three. Once in place and turned on, move on to step two: priming.

2. Priming with Microbe Food

Priming the system is step two of cycling. This involves adding food for your microorganism colonies. Commonly done with liquid seaweed extract in tandem with molasses, this can also be accomplished with the supplementation of rock dust, aka azomite. These foods are to be added to the sump tank and mixed in thoroughly to turn the water very dark. Allow a minimum of 24 hours for this mixture to cycle through the entire system.

3. Heating the Water

Once your system is filled, primed, and recirculated with microbiological food, ensure that your water is 50°F or warmer. This can be done with aquarium water heaters on a small scale or in-line heaters on a large scale. Check the temperature in the daytime and at night to make sure it stays above that threshold for two days. This provides the incoming bacteria with enough warmth to metabolize the trace minerals and keep them active. Any colder and they would go dormant or perish.

4. Reaching Target pH

Reaching that ideal pH range of 6.5 to 7.5 is key to hosting a successful nitrification cycle. The beneficial bacteria that facilitate the nitrification cycle do not operate at pH below 6.5, so this will be the minimum threshold for optimal system health. Once your water has warmed up to at least 50°F, measure your pH at least twice a day. If it isn't within range, add either calcium carbonate or potassium bicarbonate and continue to measure until you have a stable pH within that target for three consecutive days before moving on to step 5.

5. Dosing Bacteria

Dosing the system with bacteria is the next essential part of cycling. Bottled nitrifying bacteria (see page 23) do have an expiration date, so make sure you order them when you are ready. Follow the package directions and make sure to add the bacteria into your MBBR or media bed, depending on which arrangement you select for your system.

On the off chance you are unable to source bottled bacteria but do have access to a functioning system with an active bacterial colony, there is hope yet. If you can acquire 10 percent of the water you need for your media bed or biofilter from this system, there should be enough seed bacteria (inoculum) to spur the development of a colony in your system. Make sure that during transport there is aeration taking place to prevent die-off.

6. Fishless Cycling

At this point, you can begin to fuel the bacterial growth with ammonia in either liquid or powder form for **fishless cycling**. As always, read the directions of your ammonia product before adding it so that you can reach a target of 3 to 4 ppm. Upon reaching that level, test your water twice a day for three to four weeks until nitrates are present.

Over the first one to two weeks you will want to add ammonia to keep it at 3 to 4 ppm. During weeks two and three, your nitrite levels will begin to rise as your ammonia level decreases. Continue to add ammonia until nitrates begin to show measurable levels in your daily testing, sometime between weeks three and four. Stop adding ammonia and continue testing until both ammonia and nitrite reach 0.5. It is at this point that your water will be perfect to add fish, which we will go over in chapter 6 (see page 111).

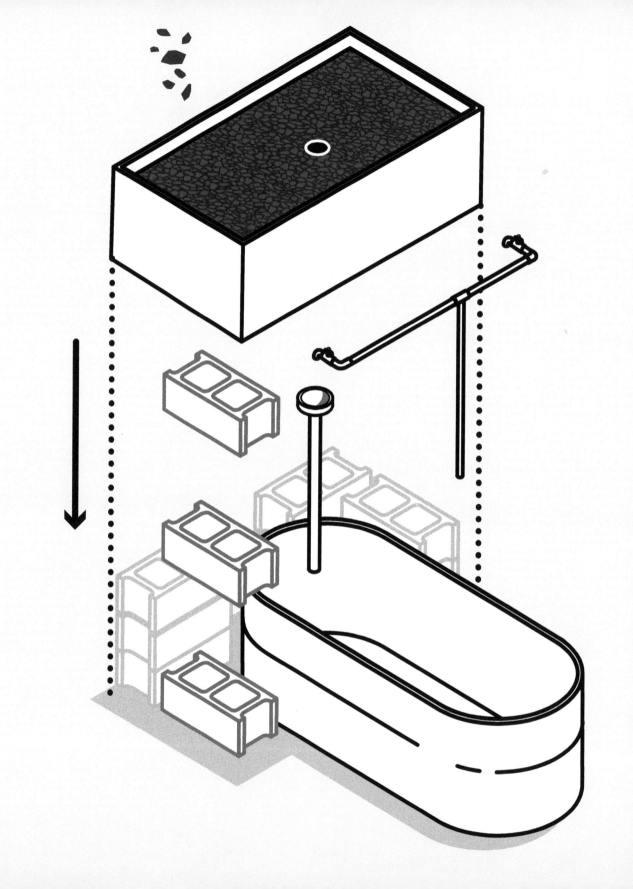

CHAPTER FIVE

DIY Systems for Beginners

Now that you have a grasp of the basic components and setup of an aquaponic system, it's time to delve into the specific types of systems you can set up to produce plants. As one would imagine, there are multiple styles to choose from, and each has its benefits and drawbacks. Some are great for multiple kinds of plants, while others grow one kind of crop exceptionally well.

This chapter outlines six different systems—media beds, deep water culture (DWC) beds, wicking beds, nutrient film technique (NFT) channels, vertical tower systems, and Dutch bucket gardens—that you can build yourself. For each system, we will discuss the materials and tools necessary for construction, as well as the time and money involved. Then we'll go over the step-by-step process for DIY construction and troubleshooting tips for solving common issues. **Each of the six designs in this chapter are for a system that will fit in a 100-square-foot area, and each grows a comparable amount of food.**

Budgets vary from person to person. I like to be as up front with my clients as possible, even at the consultation phase. I give them a ballpark cost range based on the amount of space they have to dedicate to a system and what level of equipment and optional technology they desire. As a do-it-yourselfer, you can expect to pay the following for the materials needed for any of the six system styles:

- $10 to $20 per square foot for upcycled and used materials
- $20 to $40 per square foot for all-new building materials (recommended)
- $50 to $100 per square foot if using high-tech equipment or a turnkey system

If you have a maximum budget in mind already, work backward to figure out the size of the system you can reasonably expect to afford. Divide your budget by the higher end of the ballpark range to reach your total tentative square footage for space. Commonly, I divvy up project area as follows:

- 30 percent walk space and storage
- 20 percent fish and filter space
- 50 percent grow bed space (varies slightly between systems)

No matter the system design you choose, I cannot stress enough the importance of solids filtration. For this reason, it is highly recommended that you use a media bed in tandem with systems that do not use media. This ensures that bacteria will have a place to live so that the fish can be guaranteed safe water-chemistry values. While it may be a lot to afford at once, you can begin with the following systems and build expansions later.

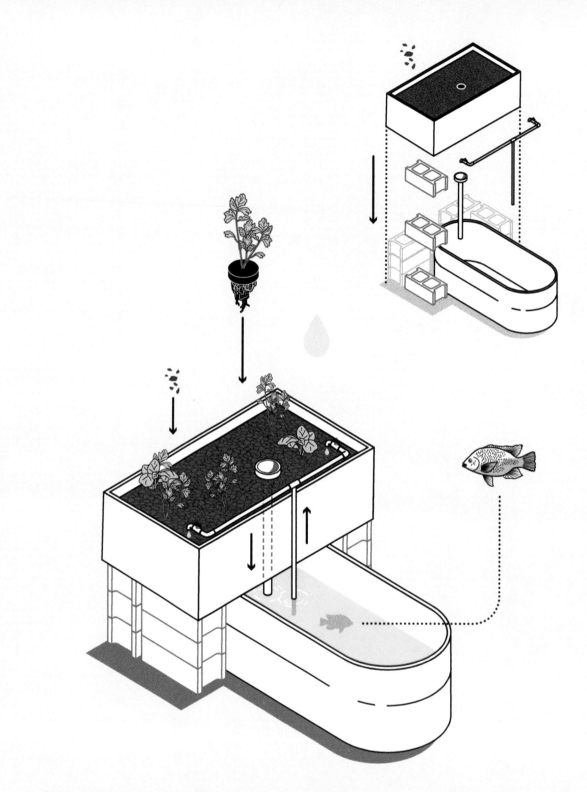

This system is designed for a 100-square-foot area. Adapt instructions on scale to best fit your space.

Media Bed System

The simplest aquaponic system uses media grow beds that are at least 8 inches (23 cm) deep. Wastewater from the fish tank is pumped up to a basin filled with heavyweight media. Solid fish waste is consumed by worms that convert it into bioavailable nutrients and minerals, while beneficial bacteria convert liquid waste into nitrate. Roots take up those nutrients, effectively cleaning the water that then returns to the fish when it drains out of the media bed.

Most turnkey systems use this method of pairing a media bed with a fish tank of equal volume. The media bed we will build is suspended directly over the aquarium, not resting on top of it, which is a common mistake that can result in tanks cracking and leaking. Media bed pairings are also referred to as "aquarium outfits" because they outfit an aquarium with a grow bed that serves as a biofilter.

What Are the System Requirements?

Media bed aquaponic systems require the bare minimum of materials and equipment to build. Here are two lists of what tools and materials you will need to construct this style of system.

Tools

4-foot level

Caulking gun

Channel locks

Chop saw or circular saw

Drill motor

Gloves

Hammer

Hole saw bit (3-inch)

Impact motor

Pencil

PVC cutters

Scissors

Sharpie

Speed square

Staple gun

Tape measure

T25 drill bit

Materials

- 1 air pump
- 3 air stones
- 1 (25-foot) bundle of air tubing
- 1 (50-gallon) aquarium or stock tank
- 1 (2-inch) bulkhead fitting
- 16 cement cinder blocks
- 1 tube clear silicone caulking
- 2 (1 × 2-inch) 8-foot furring strips
- 4 (52-pound) bags LECA heavyweight media
- 1 (6 × 12-foot) roll LDPE pond liner
- 1 (2 × 4-foot) piece ½-inch pressure-treated plywood
- 2 (2 × 12-inch) pieces 8-foot pressure-treated lumber
- 1 (2 × 4-inch) piece 10-foot pressure-treated lumber
- 1 PVC primer and glue
- 1 (2-inch) PVC screen
- Schedule-40 (½-inch) PVC pipe and fittings
- Schedule-40 (2-inch) PVC pipe and fittings
- Schedule-40 (4-inch) PVC pipe
- 1 (1-pound) box T25 (3-inch) deck screws
- 1 (1-pound) box T25 (1-inch) deck screws
- Teflon tape
- 1 (100-watt) water heater
- 1 water pump

What Is the Fish-to-Crop Ratio?

The fish-to-crop ratio of a media bed system depends on the stocking density of your fish tank. Each fish requires a 5-gallon personal bubble to feel safe and reduce stress. For our 100-square-foot template, we are using a 50-gallon tank that can reasonably raise 10 fish in an aquaponic environment. This is denser than a normal aquarium setup thanks to the grow beds converting waste to nutrients.

To maximize the efficiency of a system, I use a special ratio when designing media bed systems. Each gallon of fish-tank water needs at least 1 gallon of porous media for nutrient conversion. This means our 50-gallon tank will need at least 50 gallons of media to host bacteria that will convert fish waste into nutrients. If you only have enough space for 25 gallons of media, then your tactic would be to stock your tank half full with 5 fish (instead of 10) until you can expand.

Feeding rates depend on the age of your fish. Fry (fingerlings) can be fed 2 percent of their body weight over 4 feedings per day. Adult fish can be fed up to 4 percent of their body weight over 2 feedings per day. These are standard aquaculture rates that ensure stable growth and healthy metabolism of your fish, no matter the grow bed used.

Hybrid (Media + DWC) Grow Bed Sizing + Raft Count						Stock Density		
	Grow Space	1:1:1 Ratio	Media Bed SqFt	DWC SqFt	Rafts	Low	Ideal	High
SqFt	× 50%	Fish Gallons	/ 7.48 / 75%	× 80%	/8	/8	/5	/3
10	5	5	0.9	4	0.5	1	1	2
20	10	10	1.8	8	1.0	1	2	3
30	15	15	2.7	12	1.5	2	3	5
40	20	20	3.6	16	2.1	3	4	7
50	25	25	4.5	21	2.6	3	5	8
60	30	30	5.3	25	3.1	4	6	10
70	35	35	6.2	29	3.6	4	7	12
80	40	40	7.1	33	4.1	5	8	13
90	45	45	8.0	37	4.6	6	9	15
100	50	50	8.9	41	5.1	6	10	17

How Much Does It Cost?

Media bed systems usually cost $20 to $40 per square foot of site space. Most of the expenses go toward lumber and heavyweight media. This template 50-gallon system is pretty affordable compared to a turnkey version. Depending on where you live, taxes, and method of materials purchase (delivery or pickup), expect to pay between $700 and $1,000 for all the materials you need to build this media bed system.

Step-by-Step Instructions for a 50-Gallon Media Bed

Building a media system from scratch is pretty straightforward and takes about two days. Always wear safety gear, such as safety glasses and closed-toe shoes.

1. **Cut the pressure-treated lumber.** Using the tape measure, speed square, and pencil, measure and mark 27½ inches from one end of each 2 × 12. Using the circular saw, cut both 2 × 12s on the mark, resulting in two pieces that are 27½ inches long and two pieces that are 68⅜ inches long. Measure and mark 48½ inches on both 68⅜-inch pieces and cut them with the circular saw. Next, measure and mark 24½ inches from one end on the 2 × 4. Cut the 2 × 4 along the line and repeat the process until you have four (24½-inch) pieces. Last, cut two of the furring strips to 51½ inches and the third furring strip into two (24½-inch) pieces. Move all the cut lumber to a flat area for assembly and discard the scrap pieces.

2. **Assemble the grow bed perimeter frame.** Arrange the 2 × 12s into a (27½ × 51½-inch) rectangle. These will become the sidewalls of the grow bed. Starting in one corner, prop the long piece on its side. Position the short piece flush against the end of the long piece. Using the speed square on the inside of both pieces, check that the corner is square. Use the impact motor fitted with a T25 drill bit to screw three (3-inch) T25 deck screws inward through the outside edge of the short side to secure the corner, making sure the screws are evenly spaced. Repeat this process with the remaining three corners to complete the perimeter frame. The inside should measure 24½ × 48½ inches.

3. **Add support joists to the perimeter frame.** The four pieces of 2 × 4s are support joists for the grow bed. Insert one piece flush with the short (24½-inch) side of the perimeter frame. You may need to angle it diagonally into one corner, tip it inward until it gets close, then tap it the rest of the way with a hammer. From the outside of the perimeter board, use the impact motor to insert two (3-inch) T25 deck screws from both sides (four total) to secure the first joist in place. Repeat this process on the other short side. Measure and mark 16 inches in from each short side. Insert the remaining two joists at your marks and secure them with screws just as you did the other two joists.

4. **Modify and add the plywood.** The plywood will serve as the bottom of the grow bed that is supported by the joists. Measure and mark 12 inches in from each short side of the plywood to identify the center line. Measure and mark 8 inches in from one of the long sides to identify the center for the bulkhead hole. Use the drill motor fitted with a 3-inch hole saw bit to drill a hole on the center mark. When the guide bit comes out the other side of the plywood, remove the hole saw bit from the mostly drilled hole and flip the board over. Insert the guide bit into the guide hole and finish drilling from this side to prevent a blowout. Place the plywood into the grow bed frame so that it rests on the joists with a quarter inch of space on all sides.

5. **Cut the pond liner.** Cut the pond liner into a 4 × 6-foot piece. This is about a foot longer on each side than the grow bed frame to account for the vertical distance of the walls.

6. **Place the pond liner in the frame.** The liner must be folded so that the corners are watertight, which prevents damage to the frame. Arrange the liner to match the orientation of the grow bed. Align the center of one end of the liner with the center of the corresponding sidewall and use a staple gun to secure the liner into the top of the sidewall. Gently push the pond liner down into the grow bed and move your hands into the corners under the stapled side. Fold the excess liner in the corners into triangles, tucking them behind the inside face so that a smooth vertical fold ascends up the corner of the grow bed. Fold the excess liner over the lip of the sidewall and staple it in

place. As you push the liner down in place, move down toward the other end of the grow bed on each side, stapling the liner in place as you go. Repeat the corner folding process at the other end of the grow bed. Staple the other end of the liner in place. Cut away any excess liner that may be hanging over the edges. Use the (1-inch) T25 deck screws to attach the furring strips to the top of the stapled liner, securing it in place and covering staples. Place one in the center of each furring strip and place one 3 inches in from each end of each furring strip.

7. **Add the bulkhead.** Cut a circle into the pond liner over the bulkhead hole, being careful not to cut any wider than the hole that was drilled. Use a caulking gun to adhere the silicone caulking to both sides of the bulkhead gasket, then gently slide it down onto the flange of the bulkhead. Lower the bulkhead into the hole and press down firmly. Thread the nut onto the back of the bulkhead underneath the grow bed by hand, then tighten with channel locks to get a secure seal. Smooth out the silicone that is squeezed out of the bulkhead against the liner with your finger by following the ring shape around. Wipe any excess away on a wet rag and let it dry for 24 hours.

8. **Create an elevated platform.** Make two stacks of four cinder blocks each that measure 51½ inches from outside edge to outside edge. They should be oriented parallel to one another. Now make two more stacks oriented perpendicular to the first two, but adjoining the same side of both and separated by 19½ inches. This should form a U shape that creates a rectangle measuring 51½ inches by 24 inches that can host each corner of the media bed. With help from another person, lift the media bed up and carefully rest it in place.

9. **Connect the plumbing.** PVC pipe and fittings must be connected a specific way. Please refer to the guidance on page 47 and 48 when you see the term "connect." First, measure the 2-inch PVC pipe. Measure the distance from the bottom of the bulkhead down to the top of your fish tank below. Apply this measurement to the PVC pipe and mark. Use the PVC cutters to cut the pipe to size, then connect the section to a male threaded fitting. Wrap the threads on the male fitting with the Teflon tape a few times before feeding the

male fitting and pipe into the female threads on the bottom of the bulkhead. Wrap the PVC screen fitting threads in Teflon tape and screw them into the threads on the top of the bulkhead inside the grow bed.

10. **Create and add the media guard.** Media guards prevent media from falling into the drainpipe. Measure and mark an 8-inch section on the 4-inch PVC pipe. Before cutting the marked piece out of the 4-inch pipe, use a chop saw to carefully cut slits halfway down into the pipe, a quarter inch apart, that will allow water to enter and keep media out. Flip the pipe over to repeat on the other side while keeping the sides separate. After the slits are made, cut the pipe to size at the 8-inch mark. Use the sanding block to smooth the cuts down and remove any plastic burrs or debris that remain on the pipe. Apply silicone to one edge of the pipe, all the way around, and gently lower it in place so that it encloses around the bulkhead and PVC screen inside. Allow 24 hours for the silicone to cure in place.

11. **Add the media.** Prewash the LECA by taking the bags outside and poking small holes around them. Make a hole in the tops and use a hose to fill the bags with water. As they drain, shake the bags to agitate them, washing away dust and broken pieces. Allow the bags to drain completely, then add the LECA to the grow bed.

Troubleshooting

Of all grow bed styles, media beds can be set up to grow the largest variety of crops. In their most basic form, they serve as biofilters with higher nutrient levels ideal for herbs, vegetables, and fruiting plants. With these crops, it is a good idea to provide some support for your plants as they grow. Vines can be trained to climb up strings that you secure above the media bed. Bushes or fruiting plants can be propped up with bamboo sticks or stakes to keep them from falling over. Just be careful not to puncture the liner when setting support sticks in place.

To successfully grow leafy greens in a media bed, consider adding a solids filter between the fish tank and media bed. This creates a lower-nutrient solution better suited for leafy green production and some less spicy herbs. Leafy greens

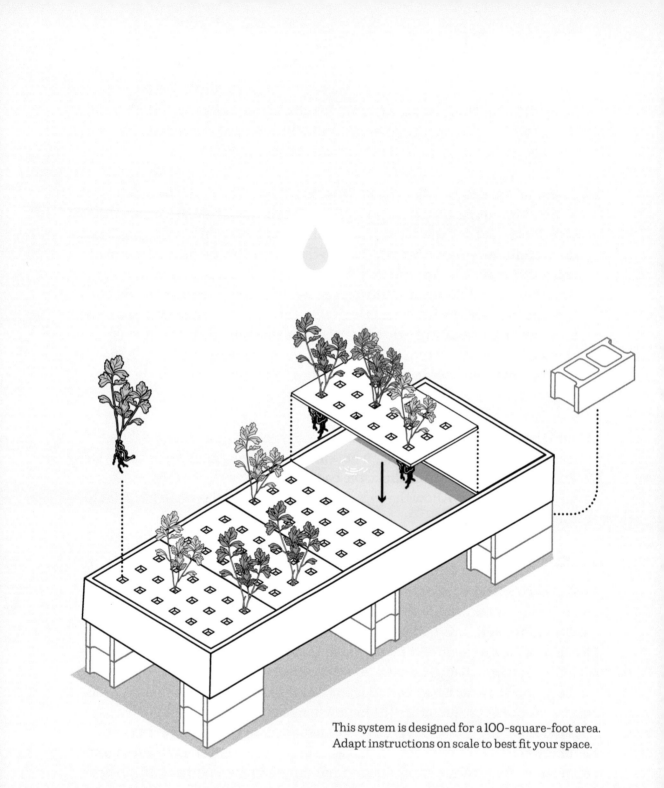

This system is designed for a 100-square-foot area.
Adapt instructions on scale to best fit your space.

tend to stay close to the surface and do not require extra support, while herbs may need some assistance. The use of shade cloth over leafy green beds helps to reduce bolting, allowing for more leaf production. If crops requiring lower nutrients interest you, consider implementing a deep water culture (DWC) system (see below) in the flow after this media bed.

Deep Water Culture Systems

Deep water culture (DWC) systems—often called "float" or "raft beds"—are used to grow leafy greens in recirculated water that is continuously aerated. Leafy greens do best farther downstream where the nutrient solution isn't so strong. The high dissolved oxygen (DO) content of DWC beds from constant aeration is often credited for good results including expedited growth and increased yields.

I've encountered countless DWC systems and found an incredibly common flaw. The inlet feeding most float beds deposits water onto the surface, which contributes to algae growth via sunlight interaction. Over time, that algae leaches nutrients from the water and can induce diurnal pH swings that negatively impact plants. Introducing water from underneath the grow bed eliminates this problem and irrigates the grow beds just as well.

Another innovation to reduce algae growth is the addition of a drain cover. Not only does it prevent algae from growing on the surface of the water by blocking sunlight, it also serves as a blocker for the floating rafts. This prevents rafts from floating over the drain and causing the DWC bed to overflow, while also eliminating the need for cutting holes into rafts to accommodate the drain.

In their infancy, most DWC practitioners made their own floating rafts out of household materials that were not always safe. Today, multiple companies make FDA-approved food-safe modular rafts that are quite durable, and these are what I recommend you use.

Measuring 2 feet by 4 feet, each raft can support either 18, 28, or 36 plant sites. Square plant sites easily host 1-inch-square plugs typically used in seed-sowing trays. Of those plugs, you can use polymerized moss, normal moss, or coconut coir. If you prefer a low-tech methodology and starting seeds with soil, simply shake soil off the roots in a bucket of water, insert them into the raft, secure them in their plant site with a stone, and you're good to grow!

System Requirements

Most of the same materials used in a media bed system are used to build a DWC system, with one exception: A filter is required before fish water can enter the grow bed. The most common option is referred to as a hybrid system, where a media bed serves as a biofilter that drains into a float bed. For this particular system, we can use the media bed from the previous section (see page 63) as our biofilter and continue the flow from its drain to feed our DWC bed.

Tools

- 4-foot level
- Caulking gun
- Channel locks
- Chop saw or circular saw
- Drill motor
- Gloves
- Hammer
- Hole saw bit (3-inch)
- Impact motor
- Pencil
- PVC cutters
- Sharpie
- Speed square
- Staple gun
- Tape measure
- T25 drill bit

Materials

- 1 air pump
- 5 air stones
- 1 (25-foot) bundle of air tubing
- 1 (50-gallon) aquarium or stock tank
- 2 (2-inch) bulkhead fittings
- 18 cement cinder blocks
- 1 tube clear silicone caulking
- 4 (1 × 2-inch) 8-foot furring strips
- 1 (6 × 12-foot) roll LDPE pond liner
- 2 (2 × 4-foot) pieces ½-inch pressure-treated plywood
- 1 (4 × 8-foot) piece ½-inch pressure-treated plywood
- 3 (2 × 12-inch) pieces 10-foot pressure-treated lumber

5 (2 × 4-inch) pieces 10-foot pressure-treated lumber

1 PVC primer and glue

1 (2-inch) PVC screen

Schedule-40 (½-inch) PVC pipe and fittings

Schedule-40 (2-inch) PVC pipe and fittings

Schedule-40 (4-inch) PVC pipe

1 (1-pound) box T25 (3-inch) deck screws

1 (1-pound) box T25 (1-inch) deck screws

Teflon tape

1 (100-watt) water heater

1 water pump

What Is the Fish-to-Crop Ratio?

Measuring the fish-to-crop ratio in a DWC system can be done in a few ways depending on your setup. Some systems will use filters introduced in chapter 4 (see page 51) to extract solid particulates in tandem with bioreactors to convert liquid waste to nutrients. Other systems will use media beds to serve both purposes. Each has its own respective methodology when it comes to fueling your fish-feeding ratio to drive plant growth.

The University of the Virgin Islands (UVI) has performed an incredible amount of research into establishing a baseline formula used in fertilizing DWC systems. They determined that using a certain amount of feed per unit of area in your grow bed was the best method instead of basing the ratio on how many plants you have. To achieve different concentrations of nutrients to grow different plant types, follow the guidelines they have established as follows:

EC	Range	Plants	Grams Feed/M	Oz Feed/SqFt	Oz Feed/Raft
Low	0.5–1.5	Leafy Greens	60–70	0.20–0.23	1.6
Medium	1.5–2.5	Herbs	70–80	0.23–0.26	2
High	2.5–4.0	Fruits & Veggies	80–100	0.26–0.33	2.6

If you opt for a hybrid system, let's expand upon the fish-tank volume formula introduced in the media bed scaling section. If one gallon of fish-tank water requires at least one gallon of media bed space to convert waste into nutrients, then that solution can fuel one square foot of float bed space. We like to scale our DWC hybrid beds to meet the growth trajectory of a given plant.

Crop	Weeks/Raft	Gal Fish/Media	Total Oz Feed/Day
Leafy Greens	4–6	32–48	6.4–9.6
Herbs	6–8	48–64	12–16
Fruits & Veggies	8–12	64–112	20.8–31.2

How Much Does It Cost?

The pricing structure on page 60 applies to all systems; components are exchanged for other items of like cost relevant to each design. For DWC, the cost of rafts and longer rolls of LDPE pond liner replaces what you would spend on LECA for a media bed. The expense of extra air pumps, liner, and stones will be the main difference. For this particular system, expect to pay between $600 and $900 for the materials if you pair it with the media bed for a total of $1,500 to $2,000. If you chose another variety of filtration, it would probably be in the same range.

Air pumps come in a wide variety of shapes, sizes, and capabilities. I like to use the Allied Aqua brand due to their availability, effectiveness, and affordability. Their lower-wattage pumps come with a six-line valve manifold that can feed air stones supporting up to 12 rafts. A good rule of thumb is 1 air stone for every 2 rafts, or every 16 square feet.

Due to the frame being nearly identical to the media's, you can expect a two-day build. If you hire labor, expect 40 percent of the final bill to cover the contractor's costs and 60 percent to cover your materials. Otherwise, stick with the DIY method and save yourself a pretty penny.

Hybrid (Media + DWC) Grow Bed Sizing + Raft Count						Stock Density		
	Grow Space	1:1:1 Ratio	Media Bed SqFt	DWC SqFt	Rafts	Low	Ideal	High
SqFt	× 50%	Fish Gallons	/ 7.48 / 75%	× 80%	/8	/8	/5	/3
10	5	5	0.9	4	0.5	1	1	2
20	10	10	1.8	8	1.0	1	2	3
30	15	15	2.7	12	1.5	2	3	5
40	20	20	3.6	16	2.1	3	4	7
50	25	25	4.5	21	2.6	3	5	8
60	30	30	5.3	25	3.1	4	6	10
70	35	35	6.2	29	3.6	4	7	12
80	40	40	7.1	33	4.1	5	8	13
90	45	45	8.0	37	4.6	6	9	15
100	50	50	8.9	41	5.1	6	10	17

Our template 100-square-foot site could have a DWC system supplied by a 50-gallon fish tank with a 50-gallon media bed measuring 2 × 4 feet that covers 8 square feet, resulting in a DWC bed measuring 4 × 10 feet to cover the remaining 40 square feet of grow space with 4 rafts.

Step-by-Step Instructions

1. **Cut the pressure-treated lumber.** Using the tape measure, speed square, and pencil, measure and mark 51½ inches from one end of a 2 × 12. Using the circular saw, cut the 2 × 12 on the mark, resulting in one piece 51½ inches long and another 68⅜ inches long. Using the same 68⅜-inch-long piece, measure and mark 51½ inches and cut with a circular saw again. Next, measure and mark 48½ inches in from each end on one of the 2 × 4s. Cut the 2 × 4 along the lines into two (48½-inch) pieces. Repeat with the remaining four 2 × 4s to end up

with 10 (48½-inch) pieces. Last, measure, mark, and cut four of the furring strips to 51½ inches. Use the scrap 44⅜-inch pieces to mark, measure, and cut two (22½-inch) pieces. Move all the cut lumber to a flat area for assembly and discard the rest.

2. **Assemble the grow bed perimeter frame.** Arrange the 2 × 12s into a (51½ × 123-inch) rectangle. These will become the sidewalls of the grow bed. Starting in one corner, prop the long piece on its side. Position the short piece flush against the end of the long piece. Using the speed square on the inside of both pieces, check that the corner is square. Use the impact motor fitted with a T25 drill bit to screw three (3-inch) T25 deck screws inward through the outside edge of the short side to secure the corner, making sure the screws are evenly spaced. Repeat this process with the remaining three corners to complete the perimeter frame. The inside should measure 48½ × 120½ inches.

3. **Add support joists to the perimeter frame.** The 10 pieces of 2 × 4s are support joists for the grow bed. Insert one piece flush with the short (48½-inch) side of the perimeter frame. You may need to angle it diagonally into one corner, tip it inward until it gets close, then tap it the rest of the way with a hammer. From the outside of the perimeter board, use the impact motor to insert two (3-inch) T25 deck screws from both sides (four total) to secure the first joist in place. Repeat this process on the other short side. Measure and mark every 16 inches in from one short side. Insert the remaining eight joists at your marks and secure them in place with screws the same as you did the other two joists.

4. **Modify and add the plywood.** The plywood will serve as the bottom of the grow bed that is supported by the joists. On the full 4 × 8-foot sheet of plywood, measure and mark 24 inches in from each long side of the plywood to identify the center line. Along this center line, measure and mark 8 inches in from one of the short sides to identify the center for the first bulkhead hole. Use the drill motor fitted with a 3-inch hole saw bit to drill a hole on the center mark. When the guide bit comes out the other side of the plywood, remove the hole saw bit from the mostly drilled hole and flip the board over.

Insert the guide bit into the guide hole and finish drilling from this side to prevent a blowout. Place the plywood into the grow bed frame so that it rests on the joists with a quarter inch of space on three sides, with enough space on the remaining side to place the 2 × 4-foot piece of plywood. Repeat the steps above to add the second hole at the other end of the grow bed as a mirror image.

5. **Cut the pond liner.** Cut the pond liner into a 6 × 12-foot piece. This is about a foot longer on each side than the grow bed frame to account for the vertical distance of the walls.

6. **Place the pond liner in the frame.** The liner must be folded so that the corners are watertight, which prevents damage to the frame. Arrange the liner to match the orientation of the grow bed. Align the center of one end of the liner with the center of the corresponding sidewall and use a staple gun to secure the liner into the top of the sidewall. Gently push the pond liner down into the grow bed and move your hands into the corners under the stapled side. Fold the excess liner in the corners into triangles, tucking them behind the inside face so that a smooth vertical fold ascends up the corner of the grow bed. Fold the excess liner over the lip of the sidewall and staple it in place. As you push the liner down in place, move toward the other end of the grow bed on each side, stapling the liner in place as you go. Repeat the corner folding process at the other end of the grow bed. Staple the other end of the liner in place. Cut away any excess liner that may be hanging over the edges. Use the (1-inch) T25 deck screws to attach the furring strips to the top of the stapled liner, securing it in place and covering the staples. Place one in the center of each furring strip and place one three inches in from each end of each furring strip.

7. **Add the bulkheads.** Cut a circle into the pond liner over each bulkhead hole, being careful not to cut any wider than the hole that was drilled. Use a caulking gun to adhere the silicone caulking to both sides of the bulkhead gasket, then gently slide it down over the threads onto the flange of the bulkhead. Lower the bulkhead into the hole and press down firmly. Thread the nut onto the back of the bulkhead underneath the grow bed by hand, then tighten with channel locks to get a secure seal. Smooth out the silicone that is squeezed out of the bulkhead against the liner with your finger by following the ring shape around. Repeat on the other hole with the second bulkhead. Wipe any excess away on a wet rag and let it dry for 24 hours.

8. **Create an elevated platform.** Make two stacks of three cinder blocks each that measure 51½ inches from outside edge to outside edge. They should be oriented parallel to one another. Now make two more stacks 5 feet away that are oriented perpendicular to the first two, but with the same outside distance of 51½ inches. Make two more stacks just like the first ones, 5 feet away from the second set of stacks. This should form six pillars that create a rectangle measuring 51½ inches by 123 inches that can host each corner of the DWC bed. With help from another person, lift the DWC bed up and carefully set it in place.

9. **Connect the plumbing.** PVC pipe and fittings must be connected a specific way. (Please refer to the guidance on pages 47 and 48 when you see the term "connect.") First, wrap the threads on the male fittings with the Teflon tape a few times before feeding the male fittings into the female threads on the bottom of each bulkhead. Add a third male fitting to the top of the drain bulkhead inside the grow bed.

   Next, measure the sections of 2-inch PVC pipe. Place a 2-inch 90-degree elbow directly beneath your media/biofilter drain bulkhead and measure the distance from the bottom of the male fitting in the bulkhead down to the top of the 90-degree elbow. Apply this measurement to the PVC pipe and mark. Use the PVC cutters to cut the pipe to size, then connect the section to the 90-degree elbow, then to the male fitting. You may have to tilt the pipe (joined to the 90-degree elbow) to get it to slip into place before twisting it. Make sure to orient the vacant end of the 90-degree elbow so that it points toward the inlet for the DWC bed. Repeat the above steps for the inlet on the DWC bed. Orient the vacant end of the 90-degree elbow so that it points toward the drain of the media bed/biofilter. Measure, mark, and cut the distance between both 90-degree elbows before adding that piece of pipe to connect the media bed/biofilter and DWC bed together.

Now for adding the drainpipe to your float bed. Measure, mark, and cut with PVC cutters a section of 2-inch pipe 5 inches long. This pipe will not be connected with glue, but instead will be dry-fitted into the male fitting inside the grow bed's drain bulkhead. This should leave 1 inch of space below the top of the pond liner, which is key to keeping the 1-inch-high floating rafts in place and preventing wind from blowing them out of the grow bed. When it comes time to fill up your system (see chapter 6, page 111) you will want to closely monitor the DWC bed as it fills up to ensure the drain is not too tall.

10. **Create and add the media guard.** Media guards prevent roots from growing into the drainpipe. Measure and mark an 8-inch section on the 4-inch PVC pipe leftover from making your media bed's media guard. Measure and mark an 8-inch section on the 4-inch PVC pipe. Before cutting the marked piece out of the 4-inch pipe, use a chop saw to carefully cut slits halfway down into the pipe, a quarter inch apart, that will allow water to enter and keep media out. Flip the pipe over to repeat on the other side while keeping the sides separate. After the slits are made, cut the pipe to size at the 8-inch mark. Use the sanding block to smooth the cuts down and remove any plastic burrs or debris that remain on the pipe. Apply silicone to one edge of the pipe, all the way around, and gently lower it in place so that it encloses the bulkhead and PVC screen inside. Allow 24 hours for the silicone to cure in place.

11. **Create and install the drain cover.** Use the impact motor with a T25 bit to fasten the fourth 51½-inch furring strip on top of the other 51½-inch piece situated on the drain end. Cut out a 2 × 4-foot piece of pond liner and staple it to one side of the last 2 × 4-foot piece of plywood. Place the drain cover atop the 1 × 2-inch frame you have created and butt it up against the doubled-up end. Put the hinges in place with one side on the plywood cover and the other on the doubled-up batten; trace in the holes with a pencil and remove the hinges. Find the right size drill bit to predrill the holes for the hinge screws with your drill motor. Use the impact motor and the corresponding bit for your hinge screws to fasten the hinges in place.

12. **Add the air stones.** Situate your air pump at a higher elevation than the highest water level in your system. Unwind the quarter-inch tubing and plug one end into an outlet valve on your air pump and guide the tubing into your fish tank before cutting it with scissors. Repeat once more to provide two lines of air to the fish tank. Repeat and guide the tubing over the lip of your DWC bed and cut it at a distance 2 feet into the grow bed where two rafts will meet. Repeat once more with the fourth line of tubing extending 4 feet farther to terminate where the next two rafts will meet and add an air stone. Add air stones to all four lines of tubing.

13. **Add the rafts.** The floating rafts will measure 2 × 4 feet and should fit perfectly in your grow bed. Place the four rafts in your DWC bed side by side over the air tubing and air stones. Move on to chapter 6 (see page 111) regarding filling, priming, and cycling your system.

Troubleshooting

Staggering your rafts to give you a weekly harvest can be difficult with limited space. Leafy greens take roughly 6 weeks, so 6 rafts are ideal, as is a 10-foot-long grow bed. Herbs that take 12 weeks will need 12 rafts in a 26-foot-long grow bed. If you lack the space or funds for that larger scale, use half a raft per week, or a quarter raft per week, to fit your limits.

The two main types of raft beds are either raised or at ground level. Raised bed frames are typically supported by cinder blocks or 4 × 4-foot lumber legs, allowing easy access to key plumbing locations underneath while also creating storage space. Ground beds require channels to be dug out to accommodate underground plumbing lines and sump tanks to be dug into pits deeper than the DWC beds. Whichever method suits your fancy, you will need to make some plumbing decisions.

While aesthetic in nature, the most common problem is algae growth on raft surfaces. This may occur from droplets on the surface or at empty plant sites. To address both, it's best to wait until after you harvest from the given raft. Then, gently scrub with a bristle brush and some soap before letting the raft air dry away from direct sunlight and storing it for future use.

Algae can also appear where rafts meet the sidewalls. To eliminate this, staple some extra strips of pond liner facing into the grow bed to cast a shadow over the raft-to-wall gap. This technique also serves as a wind block to keep your rafts in the bed, while still allowing for smooth sliding from one side to the other.

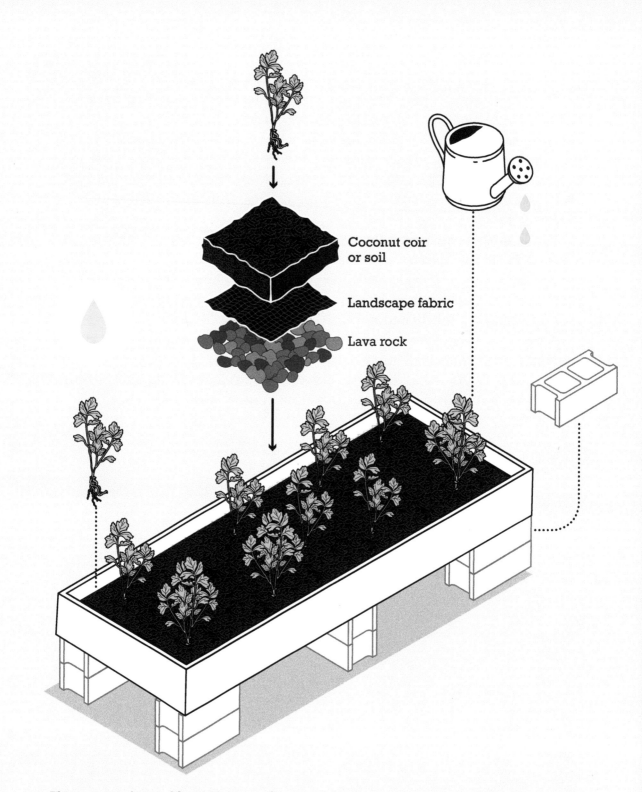

Coconut coir
or soil

Landscape fabric

Lava rock

This system is designed for a 100-square-foot area. Adapt instructions on scale to best fit your space.

Wicking Bed Systems

Wicking bed systems are made of the same lumber and liner frame as media and DWC systems, only they are designed to serve the soil-inclined farmer who wants to cultivate root crops. That's right, folks, you can use soil in an aquaponics system. However, there are a few principles to be aware of that make this possible without the detriments mentioned earlier.

These grow beds exploit evaporation and the absorption capabilities of light-weight media to deliver nutrients to plants. A shallow amount of water two to three inches deep trickles through heavyweight media. That water saturates the landscape fabric where it wicks upward into the lightweight media. Plant roots follow the moisture downward to secure themselves for a strong future.

System Requirements

One of the most important requirements for this system is some sort of permeable fabric. Landscape fabric is the most common material used to establish a wicking bed. Some people opt for using fabric pots, which utilizes a double root zone method. Either selection will still need a heavyweight and lightweight media.

Landscape fabric is used to create a barrier between heavyweight and light-weight media, instead of being placed on the ground surface to keep weeds down. This fabric keeps the two media types separate and prevents the lightweight media from ending up in drains, which could result in clogs and overflow events.

Tools

4-foot level

Caulking gun

Channel locks

Chop saw or circular saw

Drill motor

Gloves

Hammer

Hole saw bit (3-inch)

Impact motor

Pencil

PVC cutters

Sharpie

Speed square

Staple gun

Tape measure

T25 drill bit

Materials

1 air pump

3 air stones

1 (25-foot) bundle of air tubing

1 (50-gallon) aquarium or stock tank

1 (2-inch) bulkhead fitting

18 cement cinder blocks

1 tube clear silicone caulking

3 (1 × 2-inch) 8-foot furring strips

4 (52-pound) bags LECA heavyweight media

8 (18-pound) bags organic coconut coir mix

1 (6 × 12-foot) roll LDPE pond liner

1 (6 × 40-foot) roll landscape fabric (nonplastic)

1 (4 × 8-foot) piece ½-inch pressure-treated plywood

1 (2 × 12-inch) piece 10-foot pressure-treated lumber

2 (2 × 12-inch) pieces 8-foot pressure-treated lumber

4 (2 × 4-inch) pieces 10-foot pressure-treated lumber

1 PVC primer and glue

1 (2-inch) PVC screen

Schedule-40 (½-inch) PVC pipe and fittings

Schedule-40 (2-inch) PVC pipe and fittings

Schedule-40 (4-inch) PVC pipe

1 (1-pound) box T25 (3-inch)
    deck screws

1 (1-pound) box T25 (1-inch)
    deck screws

Teflon tape

1 (100-watt) water heater

1 water pump

What Is the Fish-to-Crop Ratio?

When integrating a wicking bed system into your feed plan, there are a few approaches to consider. For hybrid systems, a wicking bed is commonly placed at the end of the flow. In an exclusive wicking system, there is commonly solid filtration and a bioreactor in place before the flow reaches the wicking bed.

In hybrid system designs, we typically station wicking beds at the end of the flowchart after DWC beds. This is because their lightweight media with amendments typically has many of the nutrients plants need, with the exception of nitrogen. The nitrogen in the water wicks upward into the absorbent lightweight media, completing the formula for the plants grown there.

Wicking beds were designed specifically for root crops, which require similar nutrient levels to fruit. However, many aquaponic growers have experienced incredible success with leafy greens and herbs in wicking beds. With that in mind, refer to the UVI ratios (see page 73 and 74) for best practices.

Crop	Weeks/Raft	Gal Fish/Media	Total Oz Feed/Day
Leafy Greens	4–6	32–56	6.4–9.6
Herbs	6–8	56–64	12–16
Fruits & Veggies	8–12	64–112	20.8–31.2

How Much Does It Cost?

Instead of spending a pretty penny filling your bed with only heavyweight media, use the leftovers on a lightweight media and some amendments. Some people prefer to mix lightweight media together and sprinkle in additional products to boost yields and nutrient uptake for the plants.

Soil will likely be the most affordable option. Use fresh soil that is packaged and labeled with its ingredients, so you know there is nothing toxic for your fish or bacteria. Peat moss is the next level up in product quality and price. Coconut coir is the most expensive of the three. These are typically sold in 1.5-cubic-foot (11.2-gallon) bags at garden and department stores, in loose or brick form.

Mycorrhizae are a form of beneficial fungi that create nutrient highways in your lightweight media, connecting their root zones together. Typically mixed in as a powder or pellets, these spores grow into tiny fibers called hyphae that transport nutrients from one plant to another. A little goes a long way and often results in 10 to 20 percent increased yield.

Rock dust may sound plain, but it packs a micronutrient punch, providing a source of slow-release minerals and trace elements in the form of crushed rocks. These powders are typically composed of granite and/or basalt and are rich in metals like copper, zinc, molybdenum, cobalt, copper, iron, and manganese. Not only do the plants love it, the microorganisms use these trace minerals to boost their metabolism.

Compost and worm castings can be used if they aren't derived from any animal manure. The goal is to keep all mammalian fertilizer out of these systems for the sake of safety. Foodborne pathogens travel in animal fertilizers that can cross-contaminate plants and make whoever eats them sick. We use fish in aquaponics because they don't typically carry mammalian pathogens.

Hybrid (Media + DWC) Grow Bed Sizing + Raft Count					Stock Density		
	Grow Space	LECA Volume	Wicking Bed	Light-weight	Low	Ideal	High
SqFt	× 50%	same	Volume	LECA – Vol	/8	/5	/3
10	5	5	28	23	1	1	2
20	10	10	56	46	1	2	3
30	15	15	84	69	2	3	5
40	20	20	112	92	3	4	7
50	25	25	140	115	3	5	8
60	30	30	168	138	4	6	10
70	35	35	196	161	4	7	12
80	40	40	224	184	5	8	13
90	45	45	252	207	6	9	15
100	50	50	280	230	6	10	17

This template uses a 4 × 8-foot grow bed frame filled with 50 gallons of heavy-weight media and 230 gallons of lightweight media, fed by a 50-gallon fish tank with roughly 10 fish.

Step-by-Step Instructions

1. **Cut the pressure-treated lumber.** Using the tape measure, speed square, and pencil, measure and mark 51½ inches from both ends of the 10-foot 2 × 12. Using the circular saw, cut the 2 × 12 on the marks, resulting in two pieces 51½ inches long. Next, measure and mark 48½ inches in from each end on a 2 × 4. Cut the 2 × 4 along the lines into two (48½-inch) pieces. Repeat with the remaining three 2 × 4s to end up with eight (48½-inch) pieces. Last, measure, mark, and cut two of the furring strips to 51½ inches. Move all the cut lumber to a flat area for assembly and discard the scrap leftover.

2. **Assemble the grow bed perimeter frame.** Arrange the 2 × 12s into a (51½ × 99-inch) rectangle. These will become the sidewalls of the grow bed. Starting in one corner, prop one whole piece on its side. Position the short piece flush against the end of the long piece. Using the speed square on the inside of both pieces, check that the corner is square. Use the impact motor fitted with a T25 drill bit to screw three (3-inch) T25 deck screws inward through the outside edge of the short side to secure the corner, making sure the screws are evenly spaced. Repeat this process with the remaining three corners to complete the perimeter frame. The inside should measure 48½ × 96½ inches.

3. **Add support joists to the perimeter frame.** The eight pieces of 2 × 4s are support joists for the grow bed. Insert one piece flush with the short (48½-inch) side of the perimeter frame. You may need to angle it diagonally into one corner, tip it inward until it gets close, then tap it the rest of the way with a hammer. From the outside of the perimeter board, use the impact motor to insert two (3-inch) T25 deck screws from both sides (four total) to secure the first joist in place. Repeat this process on the other short side. Measure and mark every 16 inches in from one short side. Insert the remaining six joists at your marks and secure them in place with screws the same as you did the other two joists.

4. **Modify and add the plywood.** The plywood will serve as the bottom of the grow bed that is supported by the joists. On the full 4 × 8-foot sheet of plywood, measure and mark 24 inches in from each long side of the plywood to identify the center line. Along this center line, measure and mark 8 inches in from one of the short sides to identify the center for the first bulkhead hole. Use the drill motor fitted with a 3-inch hole saw bit to drill a hole on the center mark. When the guide bit comes out the other side of the plywood, remove the hole saw bit from the mostly drilled hole and flip the board over. Insert the guide bit into the guide hole and finish drilling from this side to prevent a blowout. Repeat this process on the other side of the plywood 8 inches in on the centerline. Place the plywood into the grow bed frame so that it rests on the joists with a quarter inch of space on all sides.

5. **Cut the pond liner and landscape fabric.** Cut the pond liner into a 6 × 10-foot piece. This is about a foot longer on each side than the grow bed frame to account for the vertical distance of the walls. Cut the landscape fabric into two (5 × 9-foot) pieces.

6. **Place the pond liner in the frame.** The liner must be folded so that the corners are watertight, which prevents damage to the frame. Arrange the liner to match the orientation of the grow bed. Align the center of one end of the liner with the center of the corresponding sidewall and use a staple gun to secure the liner into the top of the sidewall. Gently push the pond liner down into the grow bed and move your hands into the corners under the stapled side. Fold the excess liner in the corners into triangles, tucking them behind the inside face so that a smooth vertical fold ascends up the corner of the grow bed. Fold the excess liner over the lip of the sidewall and staple it in place. As you push the liner down in place, move toward the other end of the grow bed on each side, stapling the liner in place as you go. Repeat the corner folding process at the other end of the grow bed. Staple the other end of the liner in place. Cut away any excess liner that may be hanging over the edges.

7. **Add the bulkheads.** Cut a circle into the pond liner over each bulkhead hole, being careful not to cut any wider than the hole that was drilled. Use a caulking gun to adhere the silicone caulking to both sides of the bulkhead gasket, then gently slide it down over the threads onto the flange of the bulkhead. Lower the bulkhead into the hole and press down firmly. Thread the nut onto the backside of the bulkhead underneath the grow bed by hand, then tighten with channel locks to get a secure seal. Smooth out the silicone that is squeezed out of the bulkhead against the liner with your finger by following the ring shape around. Repeat on the other hole with the second bulkhead. Wipe any excess away on a wet rag and let it dry for 24 hours.

8. **Create an elevated platform.** Make two stacks of three cinder blocks each that measure 51½ inches from outside edge to outside edge. They should be oriented parallel to one another. Now make two more stacks four feet away that are oriented perpendicular to the first two, but with the same outside distance of 51½ inches. Make two more stacks, just like the first ones four feet away from the second set of stacks. This should form six pillars that create a rectangle measuring 51½ inches by 99 inches that can host each corner of the wicking bed. With help from another person, lift the wicking bed up and carefully set it in place.

9. **Connect the plumbing.** PVC pipe and fittings must be connected a specific way. (Please refer to the guidance on pages 47 and 48 when you see the term "connect.") First, measure the 2-inch PVC pipe. Measure the distance from the bottom of the bulkhead down to the top of your fish tank below. Apply this measurement to the PVC pipe and mark. Use the PVC cutters to cut the pipe to size, then connect the section to a male threaded fitting. Wrap the threads on the male fitting with the Teflon tape a few times before feeding the male fitting and pipe into the female threads on the bottom of the bulk-head. Wrap the threads on the PVC screen fittings in Teflon tape and screw it into the top of the bulkheads inside the grow bed.

10. **Add the heavyweight media.** Prewash the LECA by taking the bags outside and poking small holes around them. Make a hole in the tops and use a hose to fill the bags with water. As they drain, shake the bags to agitate them, washing away dust and broken pieces. Allow the bags to drain completely, then add the LECA to the grow bed.

11. **Add the landscape fabric.** Double up the two layers of fabric so it covers the grow bed and secure it in place as with the pond liner in step 6. This time you will be placing the fabric on top of the heavyweight media and PVC screens you just set in place. Once stapled in place, use the (1-inch) T25 deck screws to attach the furring strips to the top of the stapled liner, securing it in place and covering the staples. Place one in the center of each furring strip and place one three inches in from each end of each furring strip.

12. **Add the lightweight media.** Use scissors to open the bags of coconut coir, then empty them directly into the wicking bed on top of the landscape fabric. For coconut coir bricks, soak them in water for 10 to 15 minutes before pulling apart by hand. Spread it out with your hands and repeat until the wicking bed is full.

13. **Alternative dual root zone method:** After step 10, do not add landscape fabric. Instead, open and fill your fabric pots with the lightweight media mixture outside of the grow bed. Next, situate them in your grow bed on top of your layer of heavyweight media. Finally, fill heavyweight media in between your fabric pots to ensure no sunlight will reach the water surface and algae will not grow.

Troubleshooting

Given that this is the exception for using soil in an aquaponics environment, expect the issues that affect soil systems. Soil-borne fungi such as verticillium wilt, fusarium, and others may negatively impact your growth. Opting for coconut coir or peat moss reduces this risk, as they both allow for better airflow to root zones than soil while still being able to carry nutrients in their fibers. If you still choose soil work, make sure to have an aquaponic-safe fungicide in your pest plan.

The drain-to-waste principle takes either the fabric liner/pot wicking bed and disconnects it from the recirculating flow. Nutrient solution is deposited as remineralized solids from your remineralization tank into a wicking bed that is disconnected from the main flow. Once a week, the remineralization tank will drain out a few gallons of high-density nutrient solution that drives microbial activity and plant growth in this grow bed. This method is ideal for growing high-EC (electrical conductivity) crops like spicy peppers, hot herbs, and fruiting vines or bushes.

There are a few things to keep in mind when designing this version of a wicking bed. Drain to waste is just that: an overflow drain that sends water out of the system to "waste" into the earth. These beds do not connect back to the system. In fact, they help reestablish nutrient stores in the soils they drain into, turning formerly used-up land into arable property.

Nutrient Film Technique

The nutrient film technique (NFT) is one of the oldest hydroponic systems used today. Popularized in the 1990s, this method uses shallow covered channels or tubes to carry nutrient-rich water to root zones of plants growing in them. Ideal for leafy green production, each plant sits in a hole with a net cup and some media to keep it in place.

System Requirements

NFT systems diverge from the grow bed style, instead opting for an array of individual channels fed with a drip line. These channels are commonly made from vinyl gutters, PVC pipe, or vinyl fence posts. Drilling holes into round PVC pipe can be difficult, so for our template we will use vinyl fence posts since they are the safest to work with.

Tools

- 4-foot level
- Caulking gun
- Channel locks
- Drill motor

Hole saw bits:

- 1⅞-inch (for 2-inch net cups and inlets)
- 2¾-inch (for 3-inch net cups)
- 3-inch (for 2-inch bulkheads)

PVC cutters

Sanding block

Tape measure

Materials

- 4 adjustable sawhorses
- 1 air pump
- 3 air stones
- 1 (25-foot) bundle of air tubing
- 1 (50-gallon) aquarium or stock tank
- 10 (2-inch) bulkhead fittings
- 1 tube clear silicone caulking

1 (52-pound) bag LECA heavyweight media

100 (2- or 3-inch) net cups

1 PVC primer and glue

Schedule-40 (½-inch) PVC pipe and fittings

- 2 (10-foot) pipes
- 8 tees
- 2 (90-degree) elbows
- 10 ball valves

Schedule-40 (2-inch) PVC pipe and fittings

- 1 (10-foot) pipe
- 2 (90-degree) elbows

10 (6-foot) vinyl fence posts

20 vinyl fence post caps

How Much Will It Cost?

As with all other systems, the expenses depend on the quality of materials, which ends up falling in the same range of costs (see page 60). Instead of spending the bulk of your budget on pressure-treated lumber, pond liner, and media or rafts, most of an NFT budget goes into the channels of your choice and plumbing.

What Is the Fish-to-Crop Ratio?

The fish-to-crop ratio is treated the same as DWC calculations (see page 73), so let's figure out how many channels we need to achieve the same crop yield. With our template DWC bed being able to produce four rafts' worth of leafy greens, each raft hosting 28 plant sites results in 116. By spacing plant sites 6 inches apart, our 6-foot-long channels would have 10 sites each. This means you will need 10 channels 6 feet long to produce as much as our template float bed.

Step-by-Step Instructions

1. **Drill plant sites.** On your 6-foot vinyl fence post, measure and mark dots every 6 inches with a permanent marker. These are the centers of your plant sites. If you are using 2-inch net cups, use a drill filled with a 1⁷⁄₈-inch hole saw to drill straight down into each mark. (Use a 2¾-inch hole saw bit if you are using 3-inch net cups.) Repeat this process with the remaining nine posts, then use a sanding block to remove the burrs from each hole and clean all debris from the pipe.

2. **Drill inlet and bulkhead sites.** Use a 1⁷⁄₈-inch hole saw bit to drill a small hole between the end of a post and the first plant site. On the opposite end, use a 3-inch hole saw bit to drill a hole on the bottom side about four inches from the end. Clean up both holes with a sanding block to get rid of any debris.

3. **Install bulkheads.** Use a caulking gun to adhere the silicone caulking to both sides of the bulkhead gasket, then gently slide it down over the threads onto the flange of the bulkhead. Lower the bulkhead into the hole and press down firmly. Thread the nut onto the back of the bulkhead underneath the grow bed by hand, then tighten with channel locks to get a secure seal. Smooth out the silicone that is squeezed out of the bulkhead against the liner with your finger by following the ring shape around. Repeat on the other hole with the second bulkhead. Wipe any excess away on a wet rag and let it dry for 24 hours.

4. **Finish your channels.** Adhere clear silicone caulking to the grooves on the vinyl fence post end caps. Press them into place on both ends of the posts you have been working with, smooth the seal with your finger, and wipe the excess on a wet rag. Repeat for the remaining fence posts.

5. **Arrange sawhorses.** Set two of the adjustable sawhorses to 32 inches wide, then position them five feet apart to allow space for both ends of your NFT channels to overhang on either side. If your sawhorses have adjustable legs,

increase the height by two inches on one side. If your sawhorses are not adjustable, cut and place a 32-inch 2 × 4 on top of one to create the height difference. The lower-elevation sawhorses should be close enough to your fish tank so they can drain directly into it. Repeat this process with the remaining set of sawhorses side by side with the first pair.

6. **Set NFT channels in place.** Each set of sawhorses should be able to accommodate five NFT channels separated by two inches. Overhang the bulkheads on the lower-elevation sawhorse so they can drain easily into the fish tank.

7. **Connect the plumbing.** PVC pipe and fittings must be connected a specific way. (Please refer to the guidance on pages 47 and 48 when you see the term "connect.") Every bulkhead should have a 2-inch male fitting attached to the outside so it can feed the PVC pipe. Wrap the threads on the male fittings with the Teflon tape a few times before feeding them into the female threads on the bottom of each bulkhead. With the PVC cutters, measure, mark, and cut 10 pieces of 2-inch pipe that are 2 inches long, eight pieces that are 6 inches long, and finally two pieces that are 12 inches long.

    For the first set of five channels, use a 2-inch piece of pipe to connect a 90-degree elbow to an end channel's male fitting with the vacant slot facing the other channels. Use three more 2-inch pieces to connect the middle channel's male adapters to the middle slot of three tee fittings that have their vacant slots facing one another. Use a 2-inch piece to connect the last channel's male fitting to a tee facing upright with its middle slot facing the other channels. Use four (6-inch) pieces of pipe to connect all five channels together. Connect the 12-inch-long piece to the down-facing slot of the end tee fitting to serve as the drain back into the fish tank. Lastly, repeat for the other set of five channels with the remaining pieces of pipe and fittings.

8. **Connect the feed line.** Measure and cut 20 (2-inch long) pieces of ½-inch pipe. Use these to connect the center slots of nine tee fittings to ball valves, and nine more 2-inch pieces to connect the other side of the ball valves to

90-degree elbows that will point downward into each inlet. Rest these in place and measure, mark, and cut pipes to match the distance between each tee fitting. The last channel in the line should get a 90-degree connected to a 90-degree elbow to end the flow line. Next you will need to connect this apparatus to the water pump.

Most water pumps come with adapters that thread into the pump and receive different-size pipes or tubing. If none fit for ½-inch pipe, a ½-inch male adapter may be suitable. Place the pump in your fish or sump tank, measure the height to your sawhorses, cut a piece of ½-inch pipe equal to that length, and connect it to the adapter. Connect a 90-degree elbow to the top end with the vacant end facing the sawhorses, then measure and cut a piece of pipe that runs the length of the channels (about 6 feet) and ends at the inlet apparatus you just made. Use a 90-degree elbow to connect these two pipes, and you are ready to grow.

Troubleshooting

NFT systems are notorious for being problem-prone—everything from excessive evaporation and nutrient deficiencies to algae growth and frequent leaks. These systems can be very successful options if you take the necessary precautions and plan to fail; it's the best way to succeed. Comprehending what could go wrong before it happens is the best way to prepare and hopefully prevent it from taking place.

Long channels and pipes used to grow plants tend to heat up quickly under the sun, resulting in heightened evaporation. While a DWC bed will lose 10 percent of its volume on a bad week, NFT channels can evaporate out 90 percent of the water in a single day under hot or humid conditions. In these scenarios, the whole point of water conservation goes out the window. Increasing the angles of your channels will speed up the flow of water through them, reducing exposure to high-temperature housings.

This adaptation for long NFT channels also treats the nutrient deficiency problem common in NFT systems. On low sloping runs, water can pool around larger root zones where those plants absorb that water as it evaporates, never reaching other plants downstream in the flow. That angle increase boosts the velocity of water flowing through the channel, reducing pooling and most nutrient deficiency.

Algae growth is another factor that contributes to nutrient deficiencies. The game here is to block out light and prevent it from reaching any water surfaces so the algae cannot photosynthesize. When algae takes hold in a system, it can clog the pipes, which can result in overflows if left unchecked. In addition to that, algae can disrupt water chemistry.

Diurnal pH swings are characteristic of algae: Algae will lower your pH during the day when it is growing, and the pH will creep back up overnight while there is no light. This swing can send your pH varying a whole point over the course of a day, which can lock out nutrients your plants need during those peak times.

On the structural side of things, NFT systems have many points of contact that can each result in a leak. The more channels you have, the more holes you will need to create, fill, and seal (e.g., tiny holes in your drip line for feeding each channel; bulkheads for drains that feed a return line). Being vigilant about sealing every single hole is incredibly important to succeed in growing with NFT.

Overflows from water moving faster than it can be drained is another problem common with these systems. There are three solutions for this. First you may want to elevate your channels higher so the pump's output reduces from increased head height. A second option would be to increase your bulkhead size, and a third would be to install a smaller pump.

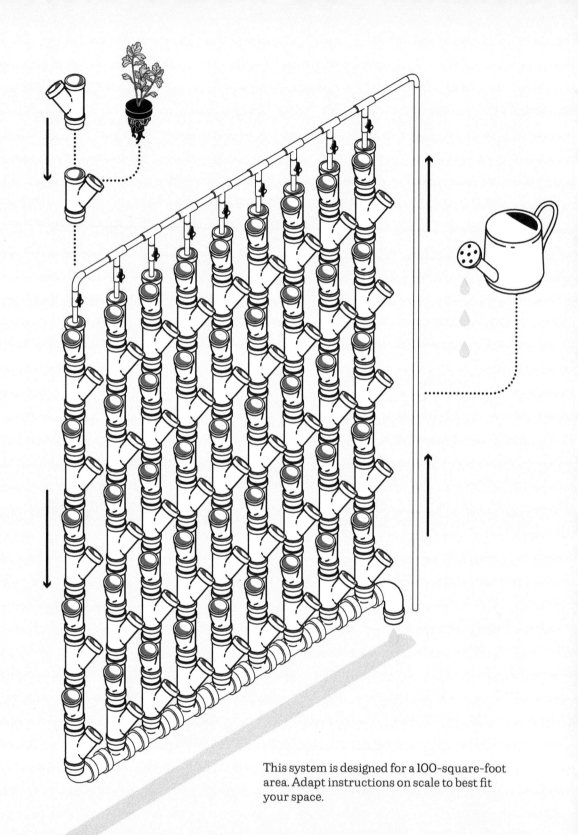

This system is designed for a 100-square-foot area. Adapt instructions on scale to best fit your space.

Vertical Towers

Tower systems are great if you do not have a lot of space to work with. They can be very aesthetically pleasing in the home and do not have to be large and bulky like the other systems we have covered. These can be any vertical farming apparatus that is outfitted to grow 10 to 18 plants per horizontal square foot by utilizing vertical area instead. The easiest way to imagine this is to flip an NFT system to stand upright and voilà: a vertical system! Alas, it is not that easy to build.

Tower PVC wye systems are by far the easiest and safest due to their modularity. A wye fitting is shaped like the letter Y except that one of the arms is vertical. This allows the water deposited in the top to drip down the central column. Net cups and seed plugs both fit nicely into the round holes if you size your fittings to match. Take a net cup or plug with you to the store when sizing your pipe housing to make sure of a snug fit.

System Requirements

System requirements for a vertical system are not too different from NFT systems. Most use the same exact materials with varying degrees of efficiency. Vinyl fence post systems have slits cut down the middle and are filled with LECA, making them very heavy and difficult to work with. I recommend staying away from those unless you get the turnkey version that uses a patented recycled polymedia and drip irrigation.

Towers made from PVC pipe exclusively are dangerous to make due to the use of heat guns, so let's not get into those. Instead I want to share with you one of the easiest tower systems to make at home: PVC wye towers.

Tools

4-foot level	Drill motor
Caulking gun	PVC cutters
Channel locks	Sanding block
Circular saw	Tape measure

Materials

1 air pump

3 air stones

1 (25-foot) bundle of air tubing

1 (50-gallon) aquarium or
stock tank

1 tube clear silicone caulk

1 (52-pound) bag LECA
heavyweight media

100 (2- or 3-inch) net cups

1 PVC primer and glue

Schedule-40 (half-inch) PVC
pipe and fittings

- **2 (10-foot) pipes**
- **9 tees**
- **2 (90-degree) elbows**
- **10 ball valves**

Schedule-40 (2-inch) PVC pipe
and fittings

- **3 (10-foot) pipes**
- **100 wyes**
- **9 tees**
- **2 (90-degree) elbows**

Another thing to keep in mind is that towers require some form of filtration. This is vital to keeping the pump(s) operating effectively and to prevent particulates from clogging the drip irrigation lines. Using any of the solids filters outlined in the previous chapter (see page 51) should do the trick.

How Much Will It Cost?

Pricing out tower systems, while still falling in the same three expense ranges, depends more on if you are purchasing a turnkey system or if you plan to DIY. A new designer system will easily cost between $600 to $1,000 apiece and provide you with 24 to 30 plant sites. These often only take up about 4 to 8 square feet of horizontal space, giving you an expense of $125 to $250 per square foot.

The DIY versions are cheaper on the materials side, but the cost reflected in hours spent building and fine-tuning the system easily add up to the same value as a turnkey system. If time is of no concern to you, and you would like to spend the same amount of money to rival a turnkey system, then you can build a rather large vertical garden for the price of one turnkey unit.

What Is the Fish-to-Crop Ratio?

As with the other methods, this depends on how many plant sites and what type of plants you wish to grow. Vertical tower systems are capable of growing leafy greens and herbs the best, although strawberries and tomatoes also perform well. To establish your grow area and get your feed ratio, just figure out the vertical area you have as you would horizontal area with a float bed.

In this template you have 10 towers measuring 5 feet tall, then you have 100 linear feet of grow space and 100 plant sites (same as the DWC and NFT systems). Linear growth space measures straight lines for row crops (not area), so we need to find out how many square feet are used in our tower frame to calculate our feed ratio with the UVI metrics. Our template frame holding the towers is 6 feet by 5 feet for grow area, so, if we use 30 square feet, we find the following feed ratios:

Wye Tower Feed Rates for 100 LFT					
EC	Range	Plants	Grams Feed/M	Oz Feed/Sqft	Total Oz Feed/Day
Low	0.5–1.5	Leafy Greens	60–70	0.2–0.23	6–7
Medium	1.5–2.5	Herbs	70–80	0.23–0.26	7–8
High	2.5–4.0	Fruits & Veggies	80–100	0.26–0.33	8–9

Step-by-Step Instructions

1. **Build a support frame for the towers.** To accommodate 5-foot towers with 4 × 1½-inch wyes spaced 6 inches apart, the frame needs to be 6 feet long to accommodate 10 towers with 100 plant sites. Most systems utilize a pressure-treated lumber frame that keeps the catch basin and towers in place while being bottom-heavy to prevent tipping over. There are many potential options to pursue, so browse online to find what works best for your situation. Just make sure the catch basin will be high enough to drain into the fish tank or sump tank.

2. **Cut the PVC pipe.** Use the PVC cutters to cut the 2-inch PVC pipe into 100 (1½-inch) pieces, 10 (4-inch) pieces, and 1 (12-inch) piece. Cut the ½-inch PVC pipe into 10 (2-inch) pieces and 10 (5-inch) pieces.

3. **Construct the catch basin and drain.** Use the 4-inch pieces of pipe to connect nine (2-inch) tee fittings together in a row with their central slot vacant and facing the same direction. At one end, use a 4-inch piece of pipe to connect a 90-degree elbow fitting with its vacant slot facing the same way as the tee fittings. On the other end, use the last 4-inch piece of pipe to connect another 90-degree elbow so that its vacant slot faces the opposite direction from the others. Add the 12-inch piece of pipe to the last 90-degree elbow's vacant slot to serve as the drain back into the fish tank. Move the assembled catch basin to the bottom channel on your frame.

4. **Construct individual towers.** Use the 1½-inch pieces of pipe to connect 10 (2-inch) wye fittings together in a row, leaving the diagonal slots vacant and pointing in the same direction. Leave the top site vacant, but add a 1½-inch piece to the bottom slot of the bottom wye in the tower. Repeat to create a total of 10 towers that each measure 65 inches when assembled.

5. **Construct the feed line.** Use the 2-inch pieces of ½-inch pipe to connect the center slot of a tee fitting to one end of a ball valve. Repeat eight more times. Use the last 2-inch piece of pipe to connect one end of a 90-degree elbow to

one end of a ball valve. Next, use the 5-inch pieces to connect all of the tee fittings together with their center slots facing the same way. Use one (5-inch) piece to connect one end of the tee fitting assembly to the 90-degree elbow with the ball valve, again facing the same way as the rest. Use the last 5-inch piece of pipe to connect the other end of the assembly to a vacant 90-degree elbow. Measure the distance from the vacant down-facing slot of this 90-degree elbow to the outlet on your pump, then cut and connect a piece of ½-inch pipe equal to that length to complete your feed line.

6. **Adding the net cups.** Add 2-inch net cups to every plant site. Add one net cup full of media at the top of the tower where the ball valve emits water. This will cause the water to drip down the walls of the tower rather than fall straight down through it. Doing this ensures your root zones will receive the water they need to grow.

Troubleshooting

The most common issue with these systems is uneven distribution between towers. With a PVC feed line, the solution is to simply adjust the aperture of the ball valves over each tower until the streams are the same. Typically, the first ball valve in the flow will be mostly closed and the one at the end mostly open. If you want to increase pressure in the feed line, simply close most of the ball valves 90 percent of the way; just be aware this will make your pump work harder.

Harvesting can be done in a few ways. You may remove individual net cups with mature plants and process them elsewhere. Another option would be to completely close the ball valve that feeds a particular tower, wait a minute for the water inside to finish trickling down, and then remove the whole tower. When it comes to cleaning towers, the latter is the best practice.

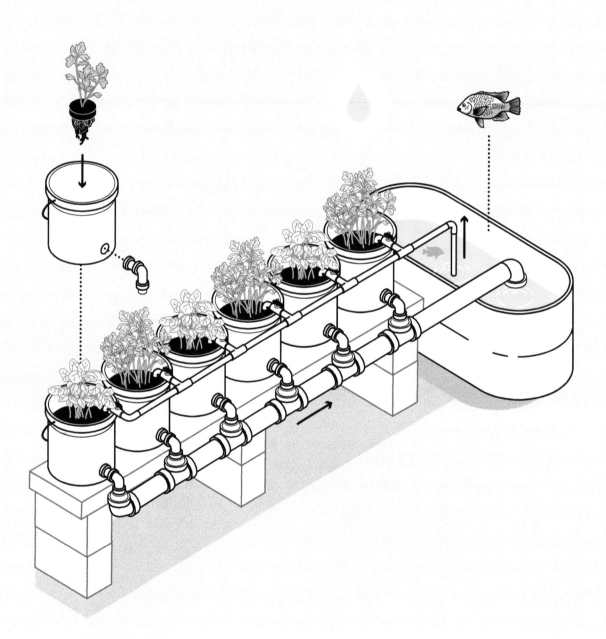

This system is designed for a 100-square-foot area. Adapt instructions on scale to best fit your space.

Dutch Buckets

Dutch buckets, also known as Bato Buckets, are one of the best ways to grow fruiting vines. A nutrient basin (or in this case a fish tank/filter) irrigates a series of five-gallon buckets that are mostly full of a heavyweight media such as LECA. A small drain in the side of the bucket ensures a shallow level of constant water exists for the plant growing inside, with the overflow being directed back to the source. Strings dangle above each bucket that are used to train vines to climb upward in a method called "lean-and-lower."

Initially used in hydroponic systems, Dutch buckets have been adapted to work with aquaponics in much the same way as NFT and tower systems. Rather than being on the ground, the buckets will need to be elevated above the plane of the fish tank, so the water leaving them can drain back into the system.

System Requirements

The requirements for a Dutch bucket system are pulled from all other facets of grow beds we have discussed up until this point. Heavyweight media is used to house the root system, beneficial bacteria, and worms. Buckets are used to contain root zones of individual plants instead of the fabric pots used in wicking beds. Optional air equipment used in float beds can be implemented to provide oxygen to the plants, expediting the growth cycle. Buckets are connected together in parallel like NFT arrays, with a catchment pipe serving as a return line.

In addition to the equipment you have become familiar with, there are some items specific to Dutch bucket systems you need to know about. The buckets are made out of high-density polyethylene (HDPE), which is a food-safe plastic. While commonly found as round buckets, I highly recommend finding square buckets because they provide a flat surface that is less likely to leak once a bulkhead is installed.

Tomahooks are a tool specific to Dutch buckets that are essential to managing fruiting vine crops. They are placed on rafters or cables in line above each bucket. Twine or sturdy string is wound around these hooks, of which the excess dangles down for the vine to climb in a process called training.

By the time a vine reaches the top, its fruit has set and can be harvested. The tomahook can then be unspooled a few feet to lower the vine until the harvested section touches the ground, creating space between the hook and the top of the vine. The bare harvested vine is wrapped around the bucket, and the process repeats a few days or a week later, effectively extending the growing season for many months.

Tools

4-foot level

Caulking gun

Channel locks

Drill motor

Hole saw bit (2-inch
   for bulkheads)

Permanent marker

PVC cutters

Sanding block

Tape measure

Materials

1 air pump

3 air stones

1 (25-foot) bundle of air tubing

1 (50-gallon) aquarium or
   stock tank

8 (5-gallon) square buckets

8 (1-inch) bulkhead fittings

1 tube clear silicone caulking

4 (52-pound) bags LECA
   heavyweight media

1 PVC primer and glue

Schedule-40 (½-inch) PVC pipe
   and fittings

- 1 (10-foot) pipe
- 7 tees
- 2 (90-degree) elbows
- 8 ball valves

Schedule-40 (1-inch) PVC pipe
   and fittings

- 1 (10-foot) pipe
- 8 (2- to 1-inch) reducer
   bushing fittings
- 8 street (90-degree) elbows

Schedule-40 (2-inch) PVC pipe
and fittings

- **2 (10-foot) pipes**
- **7 tees**
- **2 (90-degree) elbows**

Tomahooks

Twine or sturdy string

How Much Will It Cost?

This modular system can be easily scaled to fit any size operation. There are turn-key kits available for a few hundred bucks, but it is easy enough to buy the raw materials and install at home for a fraction of the cost. From a modular perspective you can calculate how much it will cost per bucket. One bulkhead, one pipe screen, one bucket, four gallons of LECA, and a bucket's worth of feed/return line with fittings adds up to about $20 to $40 per bucket.

What Is the Fish-to-Crop Ratio?

The fish-to-crop ratio with Dutch bucket systems should be approached the same way as a media bed (see page 63). That critical one-to-one ratio of fish-tank gallons to volume of media is the bare minimum for a successful system. Providing more media than that is encouraged. This ensures there will be enough BSA to facilitate the nitrogen cycle.

Step-by-Step Instructions

1. **Create an elevated platform.** Make three stacks of three cinder blocks 5 feet apart. Place a piece of 2 × 12 on top of the cinder blocks. This will serve as an elevated platform on which to place your Dutch buckets so their drain can easily run off into the fish tank.

2. **Install bulkheads.** Measure 4 inches up from the bottom of the bucket on any side. Use the drill motor fitted with a 2-inch hole saw bit to drill a hole on the center mark. Use a caulking gun to adhere the silicone caulking to both sides of the bulkhead gasket, then gently slide it down over the threads onto

the flange of the bulkhead. Lower the bulkhead into the hole and press down firmly. Thread the nut onto the back of the bulkhead underneath the grow bed by hand, then tighten with channel locks to get a secure seal. Smooth out the silicone that is squeezed out of the bulkhead against the liner with your finger by following the ring shape around. Repeat on the other seven buckets. Wipe any excess away on a wet rag and let it dry for 24 hours.

3. **Add the PVC screens.** Wrap the threads on the PVC screen fittings in Teflon tape and screw them into the bulkheads inside each bucket. This will prevent any media from escaping into the pipe and clogging the drains.

4. **Connect the plumbing.** PVC pipe and fittings must be connected a specific way. (Please refer to the guidance on pages 47 and 48 when you see the term "connect.") Set the buckets one foot apart from each other in a straight line on the platform with their bulkheads all on the same side. Connect the reducer bushing fittings to the center slot on each tee fitting and set them aside to dry. Also do this for one (2-inch) 90-degree elbow fitting. Wrap the threads on the 90-degree elbows (90-degrees that have threads on one end and a slip slot on the other) in Teflon tape and screw them into the outside of each bucket's bulkhead. Next, use the eight (2-inch) pieces of 1-inch pipe to connect the street 90-degrees to the 1-inch bushing end of each 2-inch tee, with the end bucket being connected to the 90-degree elbow with the reducer bushing. Next, connect all of the tees and 90-degree elbows together with 12-inch sections of 2-inch pipe. Use the last section of 2-inch pipe to span the drain over the lip of the fish tank to complete the cycle.

5. **Add the Media.** Prewash the LECA by taking the bags outside and poking small holes around them. Make a hole in the tops and use a hose to fill the bags with water. As they drain, shake the bags to agitate them, washing away dust and broken pieces. Allow the bags to drain completely, then add the LECA to each bucket.

6. **Connect the feed line.** Lay a 10-foot section of ½-inch pipe over the top of your buckets. Connect a 90-degree elbow to the very end and situate it over

the center of the last bucket. Move to the center of the next bucket over and use the PVC cutters to cut the pipe in the middle. Connect a tee fitting here with the center slot vacant and repeat the process for every consecutive bucket until you reach the end section that will overhang the fish tank. Connect a 90-degree elbow here and add a pipe that spans the distance from the vacant slot down to the adapter on your pump. Now, use the 2-inch pieces of ½-inch pipe to connect ½-inch ball valves to the tee fitting on top of every bucket and to the 90-degree elbow on the last one so you can regulate the flow into each bucket.

7. **Hang the climbing line.** Above each bucket, suspend the twine or string from a hook in the ceiling. Alternatively, use tall bamboo sticks in the media or other trellis material to provide a vertical guide to help the plant grow upward toward the light rather than out and across the floor.

Troubleshooting

The main issues with Dutch buckets end up being limited to what crops can be grown. Growing only fruiting vines requires a lot of nutrients and, in our case, fish feed. Since leafy greens and herbs do not do well in these systems, it creates a large profit-to-loss disparity that doesn't make growing those crops economical with Dutch buckets.

Another common issue is leaks in the form of puddles. When connecting your buckets together, it is imperative to use PVC primer and glue at every location where pipe meets fitting and use Teflon tape wherever threads meet. The same goes for allowing silicone sealant on bulkheads time to cure. Skipping any of those steps always results in leaks, whether slow or steady. Puddles invite waterborne pathogens, pests, evaporation, increased humidity, and an occupational hazard that could result in personal injury.

Fruiting vines also need a lot of fuel to grow successfully. The more we feed the fish, the more water amendments we need to add. All of this adds up quickly, and you can find yourself wondering where all that money went. This is where the cheap up-front costs of these systems level out with the other types of grow beds. That money you saved went into buying fish feed and nutrients to keep your plants happy and productive, which we cover in the next chapter.

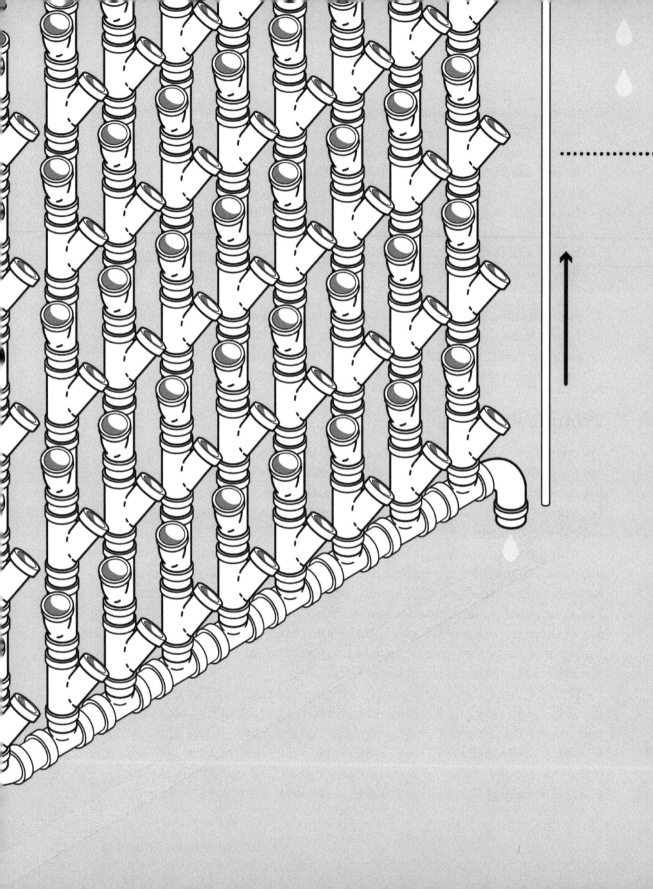

CHAPTER SIX

General Maintenance

Developing a regular maintenance routine that works for you is going to determine any system's level of success. Luckily you have this handy book to give you a head start! While the first month is intensive in terms of water chemistry getting the system cycled, general maintenance is pretty easy—certainly less time-consuming than traditional farming—as long as you stick with it.

This chapter provides maintenance guidelines and helpful tips to make your aquaponic adventure full of discovery and not disaster. Armed with a reference sheet of daily, weekly, monthly, and annual oversight and maintenance tasks, you'll be able to keep an eye on pests, identify and correct deficiencies, and care for your fish. This chapter helps you establish your aquaponic success routine.

Key Terms

- Acclimation
- Biocontrols
- Chemical controls
- Cultural controls
- Ikijime

- Integrated pest management (IPM)
- Mechanical controls
- Nojime

Diseases, Pest Management, and Plant Deficiencies

Every aquaponic system is vulnerable to infection by pests, pathogens, and plight. Because systems are often tailored to grow a few specific plants, each creates the ideal environment for pests associated with that crop. It is essential that you set yourself up with some form of **integrated pest management (IPM)**, an often-overlooked aspect of aquaponics. A practical IPM strategy anticipates pests and prepares for action with corrective measures.

Control Methods

We combat pests with the use of cultural, mechanical, biological, and chemical controls. **Cultural controls** are intended to eliminate vectors that could introduce a pest to a system. For example, you may wash your hands, change your clothes, or put on gloves before working in your system to avoid contaminating it with invisible pathogens.

Outdoor growers must protect their system from creatures visible to the naked eye. Larger mammals, such as deer and raccoons, can forage your grown goods—including fish!—right out of the system. Birds can easily fly up to a system and pick away at its bounty, just as squirrels can climb. Not only can they eat your food, but they may double as a vector that could introduce smaller organisms and organic matter to your system. Incorporating cultural controls such as fencing, netting, or low tunnel crop covers is highly recommended. Moving a system indoors is another good cultural control method.

Mechanical controls are used to physically kill or deter pests. Small rodents, for example, can make their way into your greenhouse or home through cracks, so placing a rodent trap near this space may be the best option if blocking the hole is not viable. Snails are mostly an outdoor nuisance that are easily deterred using raised beds and copper. On this scale, we can set traps to catch them, the lethality of which is up to you, the grower.

Let's not forget the wide world of insects and arachnids. In general, there are a few effective ways to mitigate the inevitability of these pests. First and foremost is cultural control performed as daily observation and record-keeping. Inspect the undersides of leaves and stunted new growth for bugs. After identification, you can implement the ever-so-common mechanical controls of squishing bugs by hand or detaching and carefully disposing of the infected leaf. Make sure to always use shears for a clean cut as close to the base of the infected leaf as possible. This prevents tears in the tissue that could make a plant more susceptible to infection.

Biocontrols are predatory pests that hunt and consume the pest causing problems. These predatory insects are best used with indoor systems due to their potential of causing ecological damage if they were released outdoors as an invasive species. A prime example is using ladybugs and praying mantises to hunt aphids. You can find an insectary online that can match a biocontrol to your pest and mail them to you. This is a fantastic resource many people are not aware of.

If cultural, mechanical, and biocontrols are all not effective, you are left to select a viable chemical control. **Chemical controls** for aquaponic systems should *always* be certified by the Organic Materials Review Institute (OMRI). This organization strictly examines and certifies that all inputs used to make the control substance were derived from organic sources. Many OMRI-certified products even have directions on their labels for use in aquaponic systems. Fish and bacteria are very sensitive to certain organic compounds used in these products, so please read the label before using.

Use chemical controls carefully. Synthetic fertilizers derived from oil and petrochemicals will kill your beneficial bacteria and fish, creating a cascade of negative results that can be difficult to recover from. Dead organisms will rot, degrade water quality, and eventually kill your plants. If using an outdoor system, beware of neighbors tenting their homes for pests, as the fumes have been known to drift from yard to yard and affect aquaponic systems (see chapter 3, page 31).

Nutrient Deficiencies

When a plant is lacking a certain nutrient, it exhibits observable symptoms, such as yellowing or bronzing on different parts of the leaves, that you can easily recognize with the naked eye and tend to. As with chemical controls, all inputs for an aquaponic system should be organic. Some deficiencies look alike but can be properly identified by cross-referencing your water-chemistry data. All nutrients should be available within the pH range of 6.5 to 7.5. Any higher or lower and you will experience a "lockout," where plant cell receptors close and are unable to absorb a particular nutrient.

Beneficial bacteria that facilitate the nitrification cycle (see page 25) need to be in this pH range. You can add either calcium carbonate or potassium bicarbonate to reach the target pH range (see page 55).

The easiest way to tell what deficiencies your plants are experiencing (if any) is to look at the leaves and "read" them. Young and old leaves will tell you what nutrients they do and don't have access to.

If you stick to a regular maintenance routine, you will rarely experience problems, but if you stray or tend infrequently, you may see issues more often.

Stocking Fish for Your Goals

Determining your fish stocking density depends on the needs of your plants and size of your system. For a small system, aim to give each fish a five-gallon personal bubble, and for a larger system, shoot for three to five gallons per fish with ample oxygenation. If your fish will grow over one pound, provide them with five to eight gallons each.

If your grow space is suited to a full stocking density, you can use the maximum number of fish as needed. For systems that fall short in the grow space category, there is a simple fix: You can reduce the stocking density proportionately. This way, if you scale up in the future by adding more grow beds, you won't have to get a larger fish tank—you can just add more fish.

For example, if you have a 50-gallon fish tank, but only 25 gallons of media (50 percent of what is needed for proper nutrient conversion), then you should stock your tank at half the recommended density. This would mean using 5 fish instead of 10. In the future, if you add another 25-gallon media bed, you can add the remaining 5 fish to reach your ideal stocking density.

Transporting Fish

If you are interested in growing edible fish, you will most likely have to source them from a local fish farm. If you go this route, you'll a need a few things for safe transportation, including:

- A large enough cooler to hold the number of fish you are purchasing
- An air pump, line, and stones to keep the cooler supplied with air while in transit
- A DC to AC inverter to plug the air pump into your car power outlet

At the fish farm, the farmhand will most likely fill your cooler with pond water. This ensures the fish will be in the same water they are used to, reducing the risk of shock. The farmhand will load the fish into your cooler, and together you'll move it carefully to your vehicle.

You may be able to source edible and pet fish from online sources. These businesses will ship fish right to your door, which eliminates the hassle of transportation. Either way, you must acclimate your fish to the system water before introducing them into your aquaponic system.

Introducing Fish

New fish must acclimate to the conditions of their new home before they enter it. Like us, fish are very sensitive to sudden changes in their environment. Imagine you are on a tropical beach in the middle of summer, and all of a sudden you are thrown into a freezer. Fish will go into shock or die if they are abruptly moved to water with different temperature and pH than what they are used to, so this needs to be done slowly over time. We call this process **acclimation**.

The first parameter to match is temperature, which can be done with the addition of a heater for fish transported in coolers. Fish bought at a pet store and transported in a bag can be set directly in the tank to float while the tank water warms the contents of the bag. After your fish reach an even temperature, move on to pH adjustments.

Test the pH in both bodies of water to see if this needs to be done. If you are within 0.2 points, you should be able to add the fish. If the difference is larger, say a whole point, you will need to add some of the system water to the container with the new fish. Wait five minutes, then add some more. Wait five more minutes, then test the container's pH once more. Repeat this process until the difference is brought within 0.2 points, and then add the fish to the system.

Dispatching Fish

In general, it's unlikely that you will end up with too many fish in your system, unless you provide them with space to reproduce. Some species will breed unprovoked, but most require a special place to brood. If you do end up with excess fish, you can either sell them to buyers or harvest, process, and eat them.

Harvesting fish doesn't have to be messy. The humane way of dispatching fish is to practice either nojime or ikijime. **Nojime** is the practice of moving your fish to a container of ice water. This slows their system down until they freeze to death and is best for small fish like sardines and mackerel.

Ikijime is the process of knocking a fish unconscious with a club, stabbing the fish with a metal spike just behind the eyes in the top of their head, and stirring to scramble the brain. There are diagrams online that show you where to do this for each type of fish. This ensures a higher-quality meat, longer storage life, and as little stress to the fish as possible. Afterward, the fish can be bled by cutting into their spinal column from the top down.

Safeguarding Against Other Common Issues

When it comes to mitigating risks and solving problems in your aquaponic system, routine is key. Let's review the primary tasks that you can do daily, weekly, and monthly to keep your system on track. Keep in mind that long-term checks are just as important as those you make more frequently. It's the same as recommendations to brush your teeth twice a day but visit a dentist only once every six months to maintain good oral hygiene. Both short-term and long-term tasks are required in aquaponics to keep everything running smoothly. For detailed daily, weekly, and monthly checklists, turn to page 134.

Daily checklists are great tools to keep track of your data and system health. Logging all water-chemistry results is especially critical in the first 90 days. After that, the system should stay in a manageable equilibrium as long as you stick to the routine. Feeding the fish can double as a time to do a quick gill check to make sure they don't need more oxygen. Scanning each individual plant for signs of disease or deficiency helps you catch things quickly and potentially prevent an infestation.

Weekly checklists allow you to collect data that can then be analyzed and applied to make corrective measures. For water chemistry, this involves reviewing how your daily results have changed over the week. Based on that result, you can apply the necessary amendments to correct any imbalances. Draining solids from filters, turning compost, and performing a quick security check should also be done weekly. On the plant side of things, record what seeds you sowed, germinated, transplanted, and harvested by quantity and/or weight. This is also a good time to do inventory and record what you are low on so you can order supplies as needed.

Setting one day aside every month to go over your monthly checklist helps keep your eyes on the prize. From reviewing weekly and daily data, you can learn what works, what doesn't, and how much your system is making or losing. At this scale, you can begin to recognize trends in your water chemistry, identify spending habits, and formulate long-term solutions or changes.

Take some time once a year to look over your completed monthly checklists and answer some basic questions. Whether or not this is your business, treat it as such. Tracking your production costs per unit, for example, will provide insight into where you can buy better-quality goods or more energy-efficient equipment. Most rewarding of all, you'll see how much of your investment has been recouped in bounty.

If you do not have the time to maintain your system, then perhaps you should consider some automation. There are recording probes for most water-chemistry parameters that connect to controllers and can be programmed to dose your system when it becomes imbalanced. These systems can also produce detailed daily, weekly, and monthly reports for you. For most, the high cost of these units is a barrier to entry, and there is now a booming DIY community for the tech-savvy aquapon to pursue.

CHAPTER SEVEN

Growing Beyond Your First Harvest

Congratulations! By working through the previous chapters, you will have absorbed enough knowledge through experience to scale up. Having grown accustomed to regular routines, like system dosing cycles, data recording, and planting schedules, you now have the necessary skills to consider a larger operation. Whether you intend on doubling your grow space or starting a business, this chapter will empower you to go in either direction.

This chapter introduces you to new skills that are intended to refine your perspective and see systems from another angle: efficacy. In which ways can you expand your system? How do you start growing for other people? Is further automation really worth it? What does it take to run a farm business? What happens if you mess up? Answers to these questions and more lay before you.

Key Terms

- Cost of goods sold (COGS)

- Daily light integral (DLI)

- Fluorescent lights

- Food Safety Modernization Act (FSMA)

- Good agricultural practices (GAP)

- High-intensity discharge (HID) lamp

- Internal audit

- Liability insurance

- Light-emitting diode (LED)

- Nutrition Labeling and Education Act (NLEA)

- Photosynthetically active radiation (PAR)

- Retail pricing

- Wholesale pricing

Best Practices for Monitoring and Reassessing

As time goes on, your recorded data will begin to paint a picture of system performance. The information in chapter 6 (see page 111) and checklists at the end of the book (see page 134) serve as your data resource, unless you decide to track with a computer program or app. Every system has subtle nuances in operation based on a multitude of factors such as where you live, what plants or fish you grow, what equipment you choose to use, and what routine works for you. If you take time to review your data every month and year, you will learn a lot about how well your system performs and where you can make improvements. This is commonly referred to as an **internal audit**, and it is an incredibly powerful tool for both business and home systems.

Audits help us learn about our shortcomings and develop effective solutions. The checklists in this book work with any system, whether you build it from the directions provided in chapter 5 or buy a turnkey system from a manufacturer.

These checklists can also be downloaded from AnythingAquaponics.com to help you log everything on your computer or phone.

Contingency plans are a key part of a successful aquaponic operation and are necessary if you want to expand. When made in the planning process (see "SMART Goals for Your Aquaponic System," page 34), contingency plans prepare you with corrective measures for any given scenario, especially unexpected incidents like natural disasters. For example, an earthquake can spill large volumes of water and displace components from plumbing. What would you do to prepare your system for such an event? What would you do if those measures failed as a plan B?

To get started with your contingency plans, answer the following questions and then expand this list based on the additional risks associated with your location and setup.

- What natural disasters are known to happen in my location (e.g., earthquakes, hurricanes, blizzards, floods, etc.)?

- What steps should be taken during each applicable disaster?

- Where is your water and electricity coming from, and how do you turn it off/on?

- Do you have a backup generator? If so, where? Is it electric or gas?

- Do you have duplicates of frequently used equipment on hand, like gloves, pumps, and nets?

Scaling Up Your Aquaponic Systems

Scaling up means different things to different people. Whether it is expanding your grow operation or improving your procedures, this is something you should plan for. Any plans you make now will probably change as you learn the subtle nuances of your system and come to understand what works and what doesn't with the crops you choose to grow.

To scale up physically, there are many options. For example, you can double the size of your operation with new grow beds, or you can make improvements to your system, such as installing a new type of filter or incorporating supplemental lighting.

If you used the recommended checklists in chapter 3 (see page 38), you should already have an idea of how you wish to expand your particular system. Maybe those ideas have evolved into something more refined and specific. No matter what you decide to buy, make sure to do your research, read product reviews, and hop online to ask questions in aquaponics forums and group pages. To help you contextualize the costs of different equipment when considering improvements, please refer to the following table.

Scaling Up with Equipment				
$100	New or Better-Quality Amendments	**$500**	Compost Brewer	
	Extra Air or Water Pump		HID Grow Lights	
	Seeding Equipment		Light Controller	
	Grow/Germination Media		Air Flow Fans	
	Fabric Pots		IPM Regimen	
	Seed-Sowing Equipment	**$1,000**	Ducting Equipment	
	Water Heater		LED Grow Lights	
$250	Dehumidifier	**$5,000**	Water Chiller	
	CO_2 Equipment		Amendment Dosing Controller	
	Feed and Amendment Upgrades	**$10,000**	New System	
	pH Dosage Controller		New Location	

On the operational side of things, consider what you can improve. For example, investing in higher-quality inputs may be in order, such as upgrading your fish feed to organic or vegetarian. Or perhaps you'd like to improve your water quality by buying new monitoring equipment.

If you do not have backup equipment, this may be a wise investment. Over time, pumps, lights, and other equipment will invariably die, and you will need replacements. More uncommon situations—like quarantines and stay-at-home orders—may hinder the supply chain you rely on for fish feed and water amendments. Better to have extra equipment and supplies on hand for a quick fix than risk your plants and fish suffering from your lack of preparation. In the end, it all comes down to what you feel will improve the health of your plants, fish, and bacteria.

Pursuing Other Smart Farming Opportunities

Aquaponics often offers additional harvest opportunities that can help you become even more sustainable and make or save more money. Here are some common areas to look for opportunities in your system.

Sustainability. Everyone's vision of sustainability differs except in that they all aim to make the most of what they have. We try to find a use for every part of the plant that we can to minimize waste and maximize efficiency. One example of this would be to feed all of your detritus (i.e., dead leaf matter and trimmings) to worms for composting in a worm bin. The collected castings can then be hung in a stocking inside your remineralization tank to unlock more nutrients.

Extra revenue sources. Some plants may have multiple purposes in addition to being edible. Your detritus may have certain medicinal or textile applications. Examples can be found in the production of fabric and paper, pharmaceuticals, or naturopathic medicine that has existed for thousands of years. Many resourceful businesses that make value-added products (VAPs), like soaps, oils, and candles, often pride themselves on sourcing locally, which could be another source of revenue for your aquaponic system.

Power savings. If electricity is expensive where you reside, consider purchasing a solar panel system to power your pumps, as it may be cheaper than a year's worth of electricity. To select the appropriately sized solar setup, add up the expected power draw from all equipment—the total watt-hours or kilowatt-hours. Places with ample sunlight may only need twice the number of panels to account for a cloudy day, whereas more stormy and cold locations may need five times as many panels to produce as much power. One thing to keep in mind when purchasing a solar setup is the **daily light integral (DLI)** of your site location. This is measured in micromoles per square meter over the course of a day of **photosynthetically active radiation (PAR)**. For your plants to grow strong in a greenhouse or outdoors, they will need a certain amount of PAR. If low DLI is a problem where you live, supplementing with a grow light may be a wise solution.

Lighting. Lighting technology has come a long way since the turn of the century. Today **high-intensity discharge (HID) lamps** are just as common as **light emitting diodes (LED)**. Both are used to provide pink, orange, white, and blue light to stimulate plants at different stages of growth. HIDs are moderately affordable but expensive to operate due to generating a lot of heat; they often require extra ventilation. LEDs have become very affordable and are moderately expensive to operate. **Fluorescent lights** use electrified mercury vapor trapped in tubes to provide very affordable white light ideal for seed starting stations. There are tricks and ways to get the most out of your lights. If you begin with fluorescent lights, you can upgrade later to LED tubes that fit the same slots on the reflective hood. In a greenhouse, you can set up your lights on a timer so they come on for an hour both just before sunrise and just before sunset to ensure your plants get enough light. For fruiting plants, you may want even longer light hours.

Making Money with Aquaponics

You can make money with aquaponics if you take the time to plan. Compared to starting your own system, the planning process is much more involved because there is a much higher level of risk. As with all things in life, no risk equals no reward, so starting small is always advised unless you are working with an experienced professional practitioner. Armed with proper training, certification, and research, you can be a successful aquaponic farmer.

This section introduces the commercial aquaponic realm. We will discuss the importance of market research and identifying your end user. You will learn how to engage your consumers and ascertain if they will buy what you want to grow. We will also address legal compliance and how to best protect yourself and your customers.

How to Identify Your Buyers

The first step to identifying your target market is envisioning your ideal buyer. This means going beyond just "someone who will buy my plants." Think in detail about the people you wish to sell to, their backgrounds, and their passions. Here are a few questions to help get you started:

- Are your buyers like you?
- Where do they live and go out to eat?
- Are they other business owners, or are they individuals?
- What are their core values?
- Do they read the newspaper or scroll social media feeds?
- Do they live near you?
- How will you reach them?

How can you use this valuable data to build your brand? Excellent question! Let's say you've identified that your buyers like to shop at farmers' markets. Creating a simple survey and asking permission to distribute it at local farmers' markets can yield an incredible amount of data. Pose questions that go beyond age and status to provide answers useful to your business. Here are some examples:

- What are the top three crops they buy every week?
- What plants do they wish they could buy locally but can't find?
- Present a few sample logos and ask which they like the best.

Go beyond these lists. Add five more questions that will help you find valuable answers to incorporate into your business plan.

Best Practices for Selling Your Products

Expanding your farm to conduct commercial sales can be very demanding and challenging, particularly when it comes to certifications and compliance. Farmers' markets often only require that their sellers have a business license, obtain food safety certification, and are listed as additionally insured on the seller's farmers insurance. Grocery stores often ask for much more. This is all for a good reason: to protect everyone involved. Let's take a closer look at commonly required certifications and compliance measures.

If your goal is selling to a supermarket, the **good agricultural practices (GAP)** certification is a critical asset. This program certifies that your farm has training manuals, internal audits scheduled, a recall plan, contingencies, and much more. This certification ensures that the grocer is selling produce from a vetted company that is prepared for anything. This creates a good relationship with your potential client right off the bat by instilling instant trust.

The **Food Safety Modernization Act (FSMA)** that was passed in 2011 introduced the Produce Safety Rule. This requires every farm producing more than $25,000 in revenue to have at least one staff member who has completed FSMA training through the Produce Safety Alliance (PSA). At this training, you will learn how to make your business practices, as well as your growing equipment, food safe. This very informative class presents you with an opportunity to meet other farmers taking the same step.

The **Nutrition Labeling and Education Act (NLEA)** was passed in 1990 to educate customers on what they are buying. These labeling laws keep you poised to educate your customer on the product and your practices. There are strict laws that you will be held liable for—everything from font and label size to branding and quantity of labels per item are regulated. Every farm that sells packaged or processed goods must abide by this law.

In addition to legally required certifications, there are many optional certifications you can strive to earn and maintain. At the forefront of most people's minds is going organic. Given that aquaponics is an inherently organic process, most of you will not have to adjust much of your operations to comply. The biggest challenge is keeping up with the paperwork, inspections, and fees. Without this certification you cannot put the word "organic" anywhere on your label.

Other popular certifications are Rainforest Alliance, Vegan, Non-GMO, Fair Trade Sustainability Alliance, and Global GAP. Each has their own set of fees, applicant requirements, and rules. By doing proper research into each, you'll discover which are right for you.

In addition to following compliance laws, the best way to protect your business is with insurance. **Liability insurance** covers unexpected events that may unfold, and any major grocer will require vendors to have a minimum $1 million policy to qualify. This primarily pertains to contamination of food with foodborne pathogens that cause illness; liability insurance would compensate damaged parties and place all liability on you. Crop insurance will help you recoup any loss from human error or environmental damage. There are many other add-ons that can protect various aspects of your business, such as your delivery fleet, the value of your crops, and much more.

If you are unsure of where to start, make a phone call to find out more. Representatives at each certifier will be able to guide you through their processes to get certified.

Understanding Your Market

Marketing your product takes some time to refine, but actually selling it should take as little time as possible. Most buyers have only a few minutes to spare if they are interested in your product, so avoid using paragraphs and lengthy descriptions. Instead, opt for catchy phrases and allow your buyer to ask you the questions that matter to them. Here are some examples:

Fish Marketing Terms

→ Grown with aquaponics

→ Humanely raised

→ Locally sourced

→ No antibiotics

→ Sustainably grown

Plant Marketing Terms

- → 90 percent fewer resources
- → Bright flavors
- → FSMA compliant
- → Hyper-local
- → Live delivery
- → No synthetic fertilizer
- → Pesticide-free
- → Same-day harvest
- → Vibrant colors

How much you charge at the market depends on how much you spent to grow each crop. If you follow a regular routine and record all of your data, you should have a very fair number to rely on. When figuring out this price, take into account the operational costs of your system, not the capital expense.

Consider the expenses of the following as the **costs of goods sold (COGS)**:

- → Admin time
- → Amendments
- → Certifications
- → Delivery time
- → Electricity
- → Fish feed
- → Gloves
- → Labeling
- → Labor time
- → Marketing
- → Packaging
- → Plugs
- → Rent/Lease
- → Seeds
- → Water

To figure out your wholesale and retail prices, first price out your competition by recording at what prices their items are sold and what certifications they have. Next, take the yield of your crops and divide it into your COGS to find out how much you spent to grow each plant. Multiply this number by 2.5 to discover your wholesale price. The wholesale profit covers the costs of growing the plant you sold, the next plant you will grow, and taxes. **Wholesale pricing** keeps you in business with bills paid and the next round of supplies covered.

Retail pricing brings in profit and allows you to reach your return quicker than through wholesale. Take your competitors' pricing and divide those numbers by your per-plant COGS. This will give you an idea of the multipliers they use to turn a profit, which will help you comprehend the actual value of your crops. If you truly believe that your product is of a higher caliber than the competition, don't be afraid to upcharge a little more to reflect that value.

Legal Requirements

Every county, state, and national government will require you to jump through different hoops. Here in the United States, most states will require you to do the following:

→ Acquire a business license

→ Register with the Secretary of State

→ Receive your EIN (employer identification number)

→ Hold liability insurance

→ Have fish permits (where applicable)

→ Obtain food safety certification

→ Obtain FSMA PSA certification

These requirements may vary from state to state, so be sure to research more about what is required of farmers where you live. Considering these actions is paramount to complying with regulations that keep your industry safe, protect consumers, and assure them that your business is qualified to provide the end product.

Many commodity crops require additional certifications in order for you to legally grow them for sale. Examples are wine, hops, rice, hemp, and other plants used in making alcoholic beverages, controlled substances, or pharmaceuticals. To learn more about these, research what each product entails and enroll in some online courses if you are so inclined.

For those of you serious about growing big, I suggest taking a tour of a commercial aquaponic farm near you. If you are not sure where the nearest one is, go to my website, AnythingAquaponics.com, select the "Learn" tab, and click on the farm list, which shows you all of the aquaponic farms in the country and abroad. Your nearest farm will be able to inform you about local regulations and may even offer classes to get you started. Our farm list is continually expanding, so if you get your business started, make sure to reach out to us so we can add you to the list.

Checklists

Daily Checklist													
Water Chemistry	pH	T	EC	CO_2	D.O.	RH	KH	NH_3	NO_2	NO_3	Ca	P	
Low	6.5	50	0.5	300	6	50	4	0	0	20	40	10	
High	7.5	80	4	1000	12	80	8	2	1	60	60	40	**Corrective Measures Applied**
Today's Values													
System Tasks	Notes												**Corrective Measures Applied**
Leaks													
Water Pump													
Air Pump													
Lights													
Timers													
Pests													
Pathogens													
Deficiencies													
Wilting													
Roots													
Fish Feed													
Gill Check													
Pests													
Pathogens													
Harvested Fish													

Weekly Checklist													Corrective Measures Applied
	Notes												
Water Chemistry	pH	T	EC	CO_2	D.O.	RH	KH	NH_3	NO_2	NO_3	Ca	P	Notes
Low													Add CaCO or KCO2 @ 1Tbsp/ 100 gallons
High													
Mon													
Tue													
Wed													
Thur													
Fri													
Sat													
Sun													
Drain Remin Tank													
Xfer Solids													
Top Off													
Data Entry													
Security													
Sowing													
Sprouts													
Transplant													
Harvest													
IPM Measures													
Inventory Low?													
Fish Count													
Fish Quarantined													
Fish Size													
Fish Health													
Fish Harvested													

Monthly Checklist													Corrective Measures Applied
	Notes												Add Fe @ 0.5 Tbsp/100 gallons
Water Chemistry	pH	T	EC	CO_2	D.O.	RH	KH	NH_3	NO_2	NO_3	Ca	P	
Low													
High													
Week 1													
Week 2													
Week 3													
Week 4													
Week 5													
Average Values													
Water Chem Trends													
Utility Expenses													
Produce Yield													
Price per Pound													
Price per Ounce													
Value of Produce													
Spending Habits													
Investment to System													
Pest Incidences													
Net Difference													
Notes													

References

Barnhart, Caitlin, Laura Hayes, and Danielle Ringle. "Food Safety Hazards Associated with Smooth Textured Leafy Greens Produced in Aquaponic, Hydroponic, and Soil-Based Systems with and without Roots at Retail." Poster presented at the Minnesota Aquaponics Conference, Minneapolis, MN, May 2015.

Bernstein, Sylvia. *Aquaponic Gardening: A Step-by-Step Guide to Raising Vegetables and Fish Together.* Gabriola, BC: New Society Publishers, 2011.

Brooke, Nick. *Aquaponics for Beginners: How to Build your own Aquaponic Garden that will Grow Organic Vegetables.* Self-published, 2018.

Critzer, Faith. "Environmental Monitoring Certification Course." Washington State University, May 2019.

Critzer, Faith. "Food Microbiology Certification Course." Washington State University, March 2019.

Critzer, Faith. "Produce Safety Alliance Grower Training Certificate Course." Washington State University, January 29, 2019.

Davidson, John, and Steven T. Summerfelt. "Solids Removal from a Coldwater Recirculating System—Comparison of a Swirl Separator and a Radial-Flow Settler." *Journal of Aquaculture Engineering* 33, no. 1 (2005): 47–61.

DeLong, Dennis P., Thomas M. Losordo, and James E. Rakocy. *Tank Culture of Tilapia.* Stoneville, MS: Southern Regional Aquaculture Center, 2009.

Lau, Fred. "Mari's Gardens Commercial Aquaponic Farm Training Course." June 16, 2012.

Lennard, Wilson. *Aquaponic System Design Parameters: Solids Filtration, Treatment, and Re-use.* Aquaponic Solutions, 2012. Aquaponic.com .au/Solids%20filtration.pdf.

Lennard, Wilson. *Commercial Aquaponic Systems: Integrating Recirculating Fish Culture with Hydroponic Plant Production.* Self-published, 2017.

Martinez, Glenn, and Natalie Dias Cash. "Olomana Gardens Aquaponic Internship Program." Waimanalo, HI: February–October 2012.

Mueller-Dombois, Dieter. "The Hawai'ian *Ahupua'a* Land Use System: Its Biological Resource Zones and the Challenge for Silvicultural Restoration." *Bishop Museum Bulletin in Cultural and Environmental Studies* 3 (2007): 23–33.

Powered by Plenty, "Upstart University Modern Farm Education." Last modified 2018. University.UpstartFarmers.com.

Raymond, Laura, Karen Ullmann, and Ele Watts. *Bridging the GAPs Farm Guide: Good Agricultural Practices and On-Farm Food Safety for Small, Mid-Sized, and Diversified Fruit and Vegetable Farms.* 2nd ed. Olympia, WA: Washington State Department of Agriculture, 2018.

Rust, Michael B., Fredric T. Barrows, Ronald W. Hardy, Andrew Lazur, Kate Naughten, and Jeffrey Silverstein. *The Future of Aquafeeds.* Washington, DC: US National Oceanic and Atmospheric Administration/US Department of Agriculture: Alternative Feeds Initiative, 2011. Spo.nmfs.noaa.gov/sites/default/files/tml24.pdf.

Somerville, Christopher, Moti Cohen, Edoardo Pantanella, Austin Stankus, and Alessandro Lvatelli. *Small-scale Aquaponic Food Production: Integrated Fish and Plant Farming.* Rome: Food and Agriculture Organization of the United Nations, 2014.

Tamaru, Clyde S., Bradley Fox, Jim Hollyer, Luisa Castro, and Todd Low. *Testing for Water Borne Pathogens at an Aquaponic Farm.* Honolulu: University of Hawai'i College of Tropical Agriculture and Human Resources, 2012.

Udemy, "ATOLL PRO: Introduction to Aquaculture." udemy.com/course/atoll-introduction-to-aquaculture.

US Department of Health and Human Services Food and Drug Administration Center for Food Safety and Applied Nutrition (CFSAN), *Guidance for Industry: Guide to Minimize Microbial Food Safety Hazards for Fresh Fruit and Vegetables.* Washington, DC: US Department of Health and Human Services Food and Drug Administration Center for Food Safety and Applied Nutrition (CFSAN), 1998. Fda.gov/regulatory-information/search-fda-guidance-documents/guidance-industry-guide-minimize-microbial-food-safety-hazards-fresh-fruits-and-vegetables.

Washington State Department of Agriculture, "About Organic Certification." Last modified 2019. Agr.wa.gov/departments/organic/about-organic.

Index

Acknowledgments

Writing this book would not have been possible without the growing support network behind me. First and foremost, I must thank my amazing wife, Lia Connell, for her never-ending love, patience, encouragement, and support. My parents also deserve a huge shout-out for raising my brothers and me in a culturally rich and loving environment full of aloha.

In the realm of aquaponics, I would not be where I am today without thanking my mentors Glenn Martinez and Natalie Dias Cash of Olomana Gardens, where I completed my internship. They have devoted themselves to promoting research and training farmers all over the world. Their tireless work and innovation have changed the world.

The greater aquaponic community online does not go unnoticed. A special thank you goes out to Mathias Olssen, who runs the Aquaponics Anonymous Facebook group, which is dedicated to helping every aquapon with any question they could ever have. Most of the moderators run aquaponic farms all over the world.

This book would not be possible without the help of the incredible team at Callisto Media. Thank you everyone who helped make this book a reality, and for sharing the passion of helping spread sustainable gardening methods like aquaponics to the people of the world.

Finally, thank you for picking up this book! I encourage you to do what I did and go forth, build a system or 12, learn hands-on, and try to think outside of the grow bed. If we can grow the same food with 5 to 10 percent of the resources as soil in half the time, what's stopping us from growing other plants the same way? Why not native plants and trees, textiles, or medicine with aquaponic systems? Think about it.

It has been my pleasure introducing you to the world of aquaponic growing. Thank you for choosing this book to help you start, grow, and enjoy your life with aquaponics!

About the Author

Seth Connell resides outside Seattle, Washington. After training on commercial aquaponic farms in Hawai'i and completing multiple certification programs, he founded Anything Aquaponics in 2014. He has since become an accomplished business owner, speaker, systems designer, consultant, and author.

Anything Aquaponics provides consultation, training, design, build, and maintenance services for residential and commercial aquaponic systems. Seth also teaches urban agriculture at Highline College, serves on the volunteer board for food safety policy at the Washington State Department of Agriculture, and consults for multiple farms and nonprofits on best practices for aquaponics.